T0099894

Justice, Ethics and Morals in Switzerland and Abroad
Version 2008

Martin Zumbuehl

Justice, Ethics and Morals in Switzerland and Abroad
Version 2009

iUniverse books may be ordered through booksellers or by contacting:

iUniverse
1663 Liberty Drive
Bloomington, IN 47403
www.iuniverse.com
1-800-Authors (1-800-288-4677)

Because of the dynamic nature of the Internet, any Web addresses or links contained in this book may have changed since publication and may no longer be valid.

ISBN: 978-1-4401-2617-8 (pbk)
ISBN: 978-1-4401-2618-5 (cbk)

iUniverse rev. date 4/16/2009

Printed in the United States of America

Contents

Preface

What is the purpose of this book?
The book illustrates with examples the fatal effects of wrongdoings by weak managers of a Swiss bank driven by envy, greed and reform hostility. However, due to many market rumors the anxious top managers were more concerned of the future of their own than that of the bank. The subsequent takeover of the bank by a Swiss holding company was strategically clever but keeping the old management was a wrong decision and an expensive exercise. Subsequently the Swiss holding company invested substantially into this bank for twelve years without success. The long expected turnaround was achieved only by new decision makers in 2003. They also created quality research products proposed by the author 1989-1992 who was harassed out of the bank.

The teaching of Buddhism and Christianity condemn such despicable ethical and moral behavior being the source of envy, greed and selfishness. The Confucianism teaches the values of learning common sense and despite god is unknown it is an obligation to behave ethically correctly and pretenders are disgusted. However, bad virtues as well as harassment in the workplace is not a violation of Swiss law as uncovering of wrongdoings is „treason of internal matters" according to the president of the Swiss Banking Association and whistleblowers should not be protected. However, according to the „Economic Crime Survey 2007" of PricewaterhouseCoopers (PWC) published in the Swiss newspaper NZZ of October 16, 2007, 37% of the questioned Swiss companies are victims of white collar crimes of which 56% have been uncovered by whistleblowers. And who are these wrongdoers?

Mostly Managers driven by greed, financial incentives and dreaming of an exclusively luxury life style! May be they did not learn or did forget that trust and brand of a company can only build up by behaving ethically correctly thus preventing corruptions, losing reputation and market shares.

A famous bad example was the grounding of all Swissair planes 2001 as no airport worldwide wanted to fuel the planes as the former pride Swiss company has lost its creditworthiness and went bankrupt. The reason for this national disaster were its prominent top managers and board members dreaming to make Swissair to Europe's fourth largest airline despite that already 1996 the financial data of the company were too weak to spend billions for shaky airlines to realize the ill fated "Hunter Strategy". However, as misconduct was legally not a crime they were later acquitted by the Swiss court.

In the light of the above teaching ethical principles has become a discipline. However, no university can turn someone who is dishonest into a virtuous person. But what universities can do is teach students how to apply value judgments when issues are not black and white. Still more the book illustrates different teaching and financing methods of the universities in Switzerland, in the United States and in England, its influence in the business life, their problems and their efforts to attract talented students from everywhere. Finally the book discloses that no graduate can succeed and is a burden in the workplace without practical skills. The same is true for selfish and greedy top- and middle manager failing to run successfully banks and companies.

APPENDIX
The updated Version 2008 with appendix replaces the 2nd book 2006. It also shows how the Swiss workplace earned worldwide recognition for inventing and manufacturing high quality products selling well. This and the country's beauty, the economically and politically stability attracted many rich people and companies. To protect the increasing money flow the Swiss financial place legalized 1934 the banking secrecy. Contrary to the ethical Swiss workplace the Swiss financial place was attacked for its lucrative banking secrecy luring tax dodgers to transfer billions to Switzerland for 75 years also from countries with budget problems. 2007 the taxed and untaxed assets under Swiss management reached worldwide SFr. 5.235 BLN enabling its bankers to generate big profits by overcharging customers for partly poor service. The adoption of the OECD Standard replacing the banking secrecy on March 13, 2009, will adversely affect the oversized Swiss financial place as customers of today wish the best professional service missing often in the past. Finally the world's banking disaster 2007-2008 of presently $963 BLN incl. the triple digit losses of the two biggest Swiss banks was mostly "homemade", due to arrogance, greed and ignoring rules and warnings.

The Author
Martin Zumbuehl

I.
Introduction

What was the catalyst for writing this book?
The catalyst was the Swiss Federal Court decision of June 8, 2005 which was sent to the author by email and which sparked many questions. He studied in detail the six-sided printout outlining the grounds for judgment written by the Federal High Court. At the same time, He was also keen to seek out the opinion of an experienced Swiss financial expert. So he asked himself why there had been such expenditure in the dismissal of the plaintiff Mrs. X who has worked as a successful interpreter. But she did not get along with three colleagues in the Zurich cantonal police. The colleagues' behavior towards her not only led to her losing that position, but also—due to bad references—her next post with Credit Suisse. She could not accept this moral injustice, and she went from the District Court to the Court of the Public Prosecutors, to the Court of Senior Public Prosecutors, and then to the Swiss Federal Court where the complaint was finally rejected. The three cantonal policemen were acquitted as the Swiss Federal Court ruled that there were no laws on office harassment which protect the victim's position. In Switzerland, legal paragraphs are missing that would protect ethics and morals in the workplace.

How do courts abroad judge these cases? In the state of Florida in the United States, there are specially selected juries consisting of members of the public chosen at random by the court from driving license lists. The jurors judge not alone by law and paragraph, but also by healthy human understanding based on facts and statements. In 2005, a Spanish court condemned a married man to six months prison because of an invasion of privacy charge for the reason that he checked the electronic mailbox of his wife. However, what happens if no restraining boundaries or laws are present to control ethical and moral behavior in the workplace?

Some of the consequences the author experienced first-hand in the Swiss Bank occurred between 1989 and 1992—which clearly illustrated the negative effects of an enforced culture of silence. In this climate of fear, creativity and productivity could not develop. Thus investment recommendations were substandard and often misleading, and good staff and customers left the bank. After many changes in the board of directors over a number of years, a new management was formed in 2003, which dramatically improved the bank's research and, profitability in 2004 and 2005.

What long-term effects have emerged due to the lack of ethical and moral principles in the workplace? The temptation to act unscrupulously becomes more unrestrained! Well-known examples of dubious ethics and morals within the workplace are the billion-dollar bankruptcies of Swiss and US companies. SWISSAIR with nineteen CEO and board members, accused for misconduct but acquitted later as their wrongdoings were legally not a crime according to the Swiss law; ENRON and WORLDCOM CEOs, found guilty of fraud and conspiracy for the largest US corporate failures. Credit Suisse also lost billions 1997-2002 resulting from missing business ethics and wrong decisions by its CEO and president. In January 2009 it became public that the former Nasdaq-Chief Bernard Madoff committed frauds of $50 BLN. Working in a little office with a few employees and many business relations he borrowed billions for many years, invested it in funds, paying 11% interest but with new borrowed money. Only few people had doubts but were silent & ten thousands investors lost their savings.

What measures have prevented criminal acts and motivated people to work creatively and efficiently in the workplace? Ethical business rules, freedom of expression, no forced silence, and no cover-up of indiscretions and poor behavior by CEOs, managers and others have led to a better and more efficient working environment. As a consequence, whistleblowers uncovering wrongdoings must be protected according to the US Sarbanes-Oxley Act, thus substantially improving team work, creativity, productivity, and the reputation of the company. Examples are: BOEING with its new CEO, Jim McNerney, who successfully cleaned up and set up business ethics rules after the scandals from 2002 to 2005 to win contracts at all costs for which the company paid a fine of $615 million. Citigroup, 2005 the world's largest and best bank with a staff of 375.000 employees suffered from different scandals in Europe and Japan some years ago. After successful clean-up by the new CEO the bank disclosed record net profits 2005-2006. However, 2007-2008 Citigroup was also strongly hit by the world's biggest banking crises.

Therefore the bank reduced the workforce to 300.000, did raise more than $30 BLN in the market since November 2007, sold $45 BLN perpetual pref. stock to the US treasury and received an US government guarantee of $306 BLN for its outstanding mortgage loans of $300 BLN in 2008. Nevertheless, Citigroup could not escape from the unexpected worst recession for decades pushing the share prices to a record low of below one Dollar despite the bank did not speculate with derivatives similar to the two largest Swiss banks.

The mentioned worldwide bank disaster partially due to greed, ego, carelessness and lack of business ethics resulted in cumulated losses amounting to $963 BLN. In the subsequent bankruptcies and near bankruptcies quit a number of other large banks in Switzerland, Europe and in the USA were involved.

What do the contents of this book further illustrate and disclose?
- How successful managers who have good virtues, professional skills, excellent knowledge, clear strategies, flexibility and who encourage freedom of expression are real entrepreneurs and a big asset of the company.
- How unsuccessful managers who miss the above qualities are only administrators, reform hostile, afraid of criticism, working primarily for themselves and a pain in the neck of the staff. They are a big burden of the company.
- How people in Western Europe should learn from teaching of Buddhism and Asian values.
- How positive and negative effects of good and bad virtues apply in life, education, and finance everywhere.
- How and why other countries perform better economically and educationally.

II.
Swiss Justice

The case of Mrs. X

Mrs. X, on June 13, 2001, brought charges against three official criminal investigators "A", "B", and "C" of the Zurich Cantonal Police because of the loss of earnings, possible slander, official office abuse, and abuse of the Official Secrets Act. She stated further that from 1993 to 2000 she worked as an independent female interpreter for third parties and for the Cantonal Police. There she became acquainted with the three accused criminal investigators. But envy, jealousy, as well as desire for revenge due to their having been rejected sexually led to the harassment of Mrs. X. She was being bullied by them, thus hindering her work routines from March to April of 2000. Furthermore, Mrs. X mentioned that on April 11, 2000, investigator "C" wrote a work report concerning her. This report contained numerous untruths which led to the conclusion that she was an untrustworthy translator. These internal power games led to her loss of police appointments as a translator which she would have otherwise received. She was removed from their list of translators/interpreters. She was forced to search for a new job, and she subsequently gained employment with Credit Suisse on April 19, 2000. After "A", "B", and "C" became aware of her new job, they accessed old information regarding Mrs. X from the years 1987 and 1988. They informed a former team mate, "D", who worked at Credit Suisse within Security Services about her alleged crimes of that time. Credit Suisse accused Mrs. X of representing a safety risk, and it was proposed that she give her notice. Thus, the involvement of person "A", "B", and "C" directly caused the loss of a second job. The district solicitors for Zurich stopped the criminal procedure against the three officials on October 21, 2002. They came to the conclusion that the investigations did not provide any proof that could justify an accusation against any of the three accused. This order was approved on October 23, 2002 by the Public Prosecutor's Office of the Canton Zurich.

On December 9, 2002, Mrs. X did recurrent against this order of the Public Prosecutor's Office. She appealed at the single Judgeship of the District Court in Zurich. There the judge rejected the appeal on March 10, 2003. The decision remained uncontested. On June 18, 2004, Mrs. X turned to the direction of the Inner Court and Justice and asserted that a new willing witness had emerged who could confirm her accusations and that the procedure had to be reviewed. On June 28, 2004, the Public Prosecutor's Office transferred the affair to the district bar for further investigations.

The latter heard the witness specified by Mrs. X, and they also heard two additional witnesses. They decided on November 23, 2004 to end the proceedings and not take it up again according to §45 StPO of the Zurich Punishment Code Procedure of March 4, 1919 (StPO). With more evidence entered on December 8, 2004, which had not been available before the November 23, 2004 decision, Mrs. X appealed against the order of November 23, 2004. She now requested that the decision had to be waived, and the case had to be taken up again with the new evidence according to §45 StPO.

The Senior Public Prosecutor rejected this appeal on February 21, 2005. With state-legal complaint on March 31, 2005, Mrs. X requested that the Senior Public Prosecutor waive the rejection and instructed the Public Prosecutor's Office to take up the procedure again. If necessary, only the costs to be charged should be suspended. She was asking for free justice and understanding. The Public Prosecutor's Office proposed in its interrogation to reject the complaint, as far as it can enter into it. The Senior Public Prosecutor's Office proposed to reject the complaint.

Remarks of the author

The many letters and figures in the following chapters are abbreviations of codes in the German language of the Swiss penal law. Its purpose is not to criticize the Federal Court judges who made their decisions strictly on Swiss law or to teach the reader Swiss legal procedures. Instead it is to illustrate how much time was spent by the lawyers and the judges of the above mentioned courts in checking the large number of paragraphs (§) and articles to thoroughly investigate the plaintiff's complaint. Consequently, much attention was given to translate the "Swiss German law wording" properly in English for reference. Despite the wording of the investigation which was sometimes difficult to understand even in its original German it discloses the skills of the judges in interpreting and applying Swiss law. In fact, the magnitude of articles and decrees in Swiss law is illustrated that the Swiss Federation will enforce 215 new decrees in 2006, and suspended three times more of 2005. Simultaneously, the Canton Zurich alone will enforce forty-four new laws and decrees in 2006 and suspended 120 of 2005.

Judgment of the Swiss Federal Court of June 8, 2005
1st Public Legal Department of the Swiss Federal Court
Federal Court Judge and President
Federal Court Judge
The Clerk of the Court

Mrs. X, Complaint Guide, against
Court 1 of the Public Prosecutors of the Canton Zurich, Switzerland
Zweierstrasse 25
P.O. Box 9780
8036 Zurich

Court of the Senior Public Prosecutors of the Canton Zurich, Switzerland
Florhofstrasse 2
P.O. Box,
8090 Zurich

Criminal procedure
Recommencement of the state-legal complaint against the appeal decision of the Senior Public Prosecutor Judge of the Canton Zurich, Switzerland, of February 21, 2005

1.1.
The Swiss Federal Court considers

The victim has an actual or indirect interest in the jurisdiction of the accused only in pursuit of punishment Article 88 OG. The requirement and level of penalty of the accused is exclusively the privilege of the state, independent of whether the plaintiff appears as a private plaintiff or the pursued action was made at this request by the state (BGE 128 I 218E.1.1 with explanations). Irrelevant of missing viable evidence in the case, the victim is allowed to appeal in national law to highlight the violation of legal proceedings—the disregards of which constitutes a formal denial of justice. Legally protected interests, according to Article 88, do not arise from a legal right, as such, rather from the right to participate in such a procedure. If the complainant is the legal party, according to cantonal law, he is allowed to denounce the violation of those legal rights to which he is entitled according to both cantonal procedure and the federal constitution directly. But who is in the action not legitimized but according to cantonal procedure legal party can, for example, claim that he was not heard accordingly (BGE 128, 218 E. 1.1; 120 1a 157 E. a/aa and bb). However, if the damaged person is a victim according to 2 exp. 1 OHG, he is entitled to material-legal questions extended authentication to state-legal complaint. This is if prior to the procedure, it had taken part and as far as the decision concerns its civil requirements or their evaluation can affect. (Article 8 exp. 1 lit. C OHG; BGE; 128 I 218 E. 1.1; 120 1a 101. E.2a, 157 E.2c).

1.2.

Official office abuse does not constitute a case for a victim according to the interpretation of the Federal Court based on paragraphs OHG or to claim position of sacrifice according to the interpretation of the Federal Court based on paragraphs OHG (BGE 120 1a 157 E. 2d/aa in Pra 2002 NR. 179 P. 950). The complainant was a valid victim since she was hurt directly by the action of the officials. Her mental and emotional health was jeopardized as shown in statements and a professor's medical report of October 31, 2001. Therein, the plaintiff's mental health was taken into consideration, but it lacked substance. These problems could not be proven to be caused or aggravated by the behavior of the accused. As a result, the report is not evidence to claim that the complainant was a victim of abuse. The complaint has not, therefore, been considered. And the complainant accuses the Senior Public Prosecutor of denying justice by an arbitrary application of law, which is hardly comprehensible: the violation of her privacy (Art. 13 BV and Art. 8 EMRK).

1.3

The complainant was in the legal party in the cantonal procedure §45 StPO. The complaint is to that extent permissible thereby as it reprimands the Senior Public Prosecutor for having made a formal denial of justice which hurt her legal hearing. As the remaining conditions for special judgment give no reason for any further evidence, the complaint has to be considered in this framework and under the reservation justified belonging to (Article 90 exp. 1 lit. b OG; BGE 127 I 38 E. 3c; 125 I 492 E. 1b; to occur 122 I 70 E. c). Given that in the explanations of the complaint writing, no further information will be provided. They are not sufficient to demand legal requirements.

2.1

According to §45 StPO, a rejected investigation resulting from legal procedure can be taken up again if new evidence pointing to the complicity of guilty subjects arise. In her petition of June 18, 2004, she initiated the reopening of the proceedings. The complainant said she had a new, guide state-willing witness who would verify the accusation of official secrets. In response to this, three witnesses were asked. None of them confirmed the statement of the complainant that the police officers had given the security guard of Credit Suisse information about alleged criminal incidents in her past, which would compromise Credit Suisse's confidential information. Therefore this would lead to the termination of her employment. The complainant did not deny that new substantial clues had come to the surface in relation to her accusations which would have led to the resumption of the procedure according to §45 StPO.

2.2

The complainant claimed that the district solicitors rejected the resumption of the procedure although she informed them first verbally and again on December 3, 2004, in writing about the fact she was going to submit new pertinent proof. However, as the district solicitors decided on November 23, 2004, not to take up the procedure again without waiting the new proofs, it went against the most elementary rights of the complainant. The decision of the district solicitors of November 23, 2004, is not a subject of the state-legal complaint. Therefore it cannot be taken into account (Article 86 exp. 1 OG). The complaint cannot be considered inasmuch as it is not directed against the decision of the Senior Public Prosecutor of February 21, 2005.

3.

The complainant may have been able to escape paying legal costs if she had submitted the former documents correctly prior to the former documents prior to December 8, 2004. This would have meant that the district solicitors in their order could have examined them on December 23, 2004. However, she did not submit them prior to that date, and she demanded that the Senior Public Prosecutor had to examine these in appeal proceedings. Under these circumstances, it was by no means unconstitutional to charge her the appeal proceeding costs. The reprimand is unfounded.

4.

The complaint is to be rejected: At this end of the procedure the complainant bears the cost (156 OG). She placed a request for free justice and understanding which was rejected as meanwhile the complaint was hopeless (Article 152 OG). Therefore, the Swiss Federal Court in the procedure recognizes that in line with Article 3a OG:

> The state-legal complaint is rejected, so it does have to be considered.

> The request for free justice and understanding is rejected.

> The court fee of SFr. 1000 has to be charged to the complainant.

This judgment will be communicated in writing to the complainant as well as the Court 1 of Public Prosecutors and the Senior Public Prosecutors of the Canton Zurich.

Lausanne, June 8, 2005
In the name of the First Public Legal Department of the Swiss Federal Court
The president: The clerk of the court

Legal interpretation of law applied in case of the harmed plaintiff
The above summary of the Swiss Federal Court judgment is an example of how a complaint of a female plaintiff without sufficient legal knowledge can be dismissed. Her lawyer or third parties should have made her aware of the negative consequences of being ignorant of the law prior to her appearance before the judge. Ignorance does not protect the plaintiff. Under Swiss and foreign law, policemen and sworn-in office holders are in principle, always right until the opposite is proven in written evidence. It was, therefore, a further error on behalf of Mrs. X to take up proceedings with three witnesses. After all, who is prepared to stand as witness against sworn-in officials in an office harassment case? Added to this is the fact that the law does not uphold office abuse or harassment as a crime. According to law, the three officials are, therefore, innocent even though their questionable behavior—which led to this complaint—has destroyed her economic position. Furthermore, if the Federal Court states that the damaged health suffered by Mrs. X has no connection with her negative experiences within the office, then the Federal High Court Judges are inadvertently supporting the abuse of workers for reasons of envy, greed and selfishness-characteristics which are abundant in Swiss society.

Violation of ethical and moral rules
Harassment in the workplace is not a violation of Swiss law. In fact there is no legal definition of the Federal Court how intensive mental and physical violation of personal integrity has to be. The judge of the court ruled according to laws, articles, and paragraphs. In fact, with much material and temporal expenditure, all paragraphs and articles of the criminal procedure were checked thoroughly. A small comfort for Mrs. X could be that she was charged by the court a fee of only one thousand Swiss francs—a fraction of the actual costs. Although not punishable in the court, her past had been investigated. It was found that in 1987 and 1988 she had been involved in some illegal activities—although more than fourteen years had passed. When she made her petition to the judge, this weakened her case. She lost the job with Credit Suisse on the ground of these questionable activities despite having worked for the police from 1993 to 2000 where her past was never questioned.

However, since the states, society, and economies have experienced a profound change. The trend from production to services, encompassing 75% of the Swiss economy, resulted that today more employees have to live and work more closely together. Thus they are substantially more dependent on one another. The heavier burden on human relations leads to conflicts which were unknown in former times. This is the base from which situations that can be described as office harassment develop. It is the behavior of individuals or a group who form an alliance and over a long period of time systematically excludes another person: Usually, this happens from fear of losing one's job, from envy of successful colleagues or in order to hush up weak points and illegal practices in enterprises. Because of defamation, insulting and sometimes physical force, and so on, victims of office harassment often experience health problems with negative consequences for the economy through sinking productivity and personnel fluctuations. The result of stress and harassment is an estimated four billion Swiss francs in income damages annually in Switzerland as harassment becomes a problem for a growing number of people.

With presently forty-one Federal Court Judges to be reduced to thirty-eight in 2007 and replacement judges of forty-one to be reduced to nineteen in 2007, Switzerland has become a well organized Legal Rights state. But this is often to the disadvantage of the country, which protects the interest of state and civil servants and certain representatives of legal entities in the sectors of finance services and industry. The past, present, and future scandals in the Swiss economy were and are only possible because the appropriate foundations in law are missing. Besides, in Switzerland and abroad, law can be enforced only when wrongdoings and fraud have already taken place. The fact that a perpetrator of a criminal act is regarded as not guilty even for many years until he has been condemned by a court means that it is often too late for the victim to be properly compensated. Despite the complaint of Mrs. X being of a simple nature, all court dates and work carried substantial financial and temporal expenditure at the expense of the taxpayers. In cases heard by jury, the emphasis is not only laid on a tide of paragraphs and legal niceties, but also with healthy common sense based on reliable facts and witness statements as well as ethics and morals. As banana republics cannot afford a legal apparatus like Switzerland etc they rely on a jury. Thus the judgment against Mrs. X in these countries, as well as in the USA, might have been different.

Violation of human rights in Switzerland

In discussions with lawyers, they pointed out that law is only partially in line with human rights. Furthermore, misdemeanors against ethics and morals are not punishable because legal rights do not concern ethical and moral codes: Even despicable abuse of the mentioned virtues in Switzerland is only partially recoverable, and the increasing prosperity which nobody will go without or endanger favors the practice of ignoring ethical and moral principles in both professional and private life. Consequently, co-workers are afraid to discover abuses in enterprises and keep silent since they are unwilling to uncover them. The amount of unpunished cases is therefore almost 100%. On the other hand in the US today, co-workers and/or whistleblowers who uncover inconsistencies in companies are legally protected. This is completely different from Switzerland where according to the president of the Swiss Banking Association whistleblowers are regarded and branded as troublemakers and usually dismissed. This is not surprising as in practice in an established hierarchy the trustworthiness of even wrongdoing supervisors is often classified higher than that of the employees and workers.

Also the other harmed co-workers were two Swiss journalists, "D" and "S", who have been condemned by the Swiss Federal Court according to the *Tages Anzeiger* of April 26, 2006. "D" published the previous convictions of supposed participants of the post robbery in Zurich 1997. Since "D" received the office secrets through instigation and drew the information from an employee of the Public Prosecutors of the Canton Zurich, he was fined SFr 500. During the same year, "S" cited confidential information from the paper of the Swiss Ambassador in Washington. He was condemned for publishing secret office negotiations and fined SFr 800. In this case the Swiss Ambassador— who was dismissed later—proposed strategies to deal with assets of victims from the holocaust. However, for the judge of the European Human Rights Commission (EHRC), the Swiss Federal Court decisions were a violation of freedom of expression and against the human rights. In the case of "S", the European judge stated that confidential diplomatic reports have to be protected but not at any price.

The European Court decisions (EHRC) confirm that Swiss law is sometimes not in line with human rights. In fact, Switzerland is a "champion" concerning international human rights. However, nationally the situation is different writes *NZZ* from May 14, 2006. Besides, the Swiss Federal Government planned and the parliament has been considering for six years setting up an institution called "Instance" for human rights. Now prominent experts and politicians want to create pressure in the parliament. On the other hand—in the case of tax evasion—the Council of State, the Swiss upper house, approved quickly to take over EHRC tax regulations. The catalyst was a tax dodger who was forced to hand over his tax documents after he was menaced to pay a find. However, the EHRC judges of the European Court condemned Switzerland for violating the guarantee that no one must accuse himself according the *Tages-Anzeiger* of September 26, 2006.

Opinion of an Experienced Swiss Financial Expert
When reading the court paper, one becomes once more aware that we live in a state whose condition is reminiscent of medieval England. There are some privileged people who grant themselves rights which a normal citizen is simply not entitled to. For example the Swiss Member of Council of State "F.L" was repeatedly charged with speeding (once resulting in an accident) and drunken driving on a number of occasions writes the Sunday magazine of the *Swiss Tages Anzeiger* in July 2005. Yet he has never been convicted of any offence. The judicial system, too, has maintained old structures with emergency rights inserted during the war years. No wonder that in such an archaic system, harassment does not exist as a concept. Otherwise expressed, the leader gives the order and wants that the others follow suit even if it is legally questionable. This has been carried through the legal system with economic and social pressure. Thus governing and running the economy is easier making an excellent world for the privileged. The dot on the letter "i" afforded a manager of a Swiss private bank in St Galle to announce at a symposium at the St Galle University that slavery is, under certain circumstances, economically advantageous and therefore tolerable. Perhaps he had the extreme war emergency legal right in mind. However, if that were the case, this would be justified for the defense of democratic rights of persecuted people. However, the economy is for the advancement of human beings economically and nothing else.

III.
SWISS LIFE

1937-2003 Start and End of an Unusual Swiss Career

As a son of parents who only knew one another for a short time and never married, the author did not belong in solid middle-class Switzerland with contemporaries who could grow up, study in protected conditions, and make an easy career. In fact, at the age of twenty, the author learned that his arrival in this world has been an embarrassment. His first years up to the third primary school class were spent in a children's home near the Swiss town of Zug. The owner, Aunt Anna was strict, but she has always been his true mother. That did not suit his real mother, and so in order to be in her proximity, he had to move to Basle to stay with foster parents. There, Wednesday was the most beautiful day as the school lasted longest, and he did not have to fear beatings. After one year he moved into a children's home in Central Switzerland where he remained up to the completion of the sixth primary school class. The author regarded the German sisters highly, and he continued to visit them many years later, sometimes even in Germany. He spent half of the first secondary class again with another strange family in the Lucerne countryside. They were farmers and beside homework, he had many other tasks to complete. Therefore, he was shifted into in the Eastern part of Switzerland where he finished the first and second secondary class. During this period of his life the author felt reasonable happy, even though he had to work hard during holidays in order to earn pocket money. Because of this, he was exhausted after holidays, and his academic performance was bad. However, in the final examinations, he received the highest marks of his class. Therefore the bad ones up to that point were disregarded.

The transition from this point was a painful one. There were no systems in place to finance the third year secondary education or further study. In contrast, at the age of fifteen, the author's mother told him, "Now the life is full in your hands". However, with only six primary and two secondary classes, he had not much choice. So he became a carpenter's apprentice in a tiny village with food and board included in the package. The latter did not send the author first to school because he already had good certifications in the two secondary classes. Instead he operated as an assistant, chopped wood, repaired windows, was digging in the garden and fed two "grateful" young pigs early morning "which was the best job". The author was often so hungry that he started smoking and tightened his belt. After half a year he left this place and worked again for farmers. Following a visit of an architect he assisted him in the office and on the construction sites.

Once the author got a new guardian, things began to change again. He sent him for an intelligence test which went excellently. Thereupon, he contacted the director of the cantonal bank where he got the chance to start a bank apprenticeship despite his limited education. A number of bank employees did not regard him highly, so they did not support him as at that time working in a bank was a privilege. In the commercial school, he was no longer the head of the class—quite the opposite. But instead of complaining, the author taught intensively himself further. After the successful conclusion of the bank apprenticeship and after being recruited into the Swiss Army in 1957, He changed jobs frequently in order to train himself further professionally and linguistically. At the age of 23 the author started also to learn English without teachers in the French-speaking city of Geneva by sending the written homework regularly to a Zurich education center for correction. This was because at that time career planning, unlike today, existed only in rare cases. The most time-consuming and most unthankful work was that of a trouble shooter by investigating bank- and customer complaints and correcting mistakes in the bank's bookkeeping division. Initially, being a non-academic, the author only held position like these, but there was not much to learn. They were very different from jobs require creativity and problem-solving skills through learning by doing.

In 1969, the author was ordered by a Swiss insurance company to develop an analyzing scheme for companies worldwide based on financial figures. After one year, the new system was operative and showed easily the strengths and weaknesses of over 4.000 companies worldwide. This system was published in the book *Finanzanalyse in der Praxis* through the *German Gabler Verlag 1976*. Thereafter, he deepened his expertise and wrote numerous reports on different subjects. He gave lessons for further education courses, lessons for students at the University St Galle, and supported Swiss graduates in the work place realizing that US graduates had more knowledge of the working environment. They were practice oriented, unlike the Swiss whose education was largely theoretical. From 1981 to 1986, he was credit officer and vice president at a major U.S.

At Credit Suisse and at the Swiss Bank the author was a senior financial analyst until 1992. The motivation to join the Swiss Bank in May 1989 was creating better and new products and building up the backward research division. However, the author soon realized that he was mislead by weak and reform hostile managers lacking practical skill and professional knowledge but cultivated close contacts to the bank's anxious top management being more concerned of the future of their own. Nevertheless, motivated by good feedbacks from grateful customers, investment advisers and other division heads the author ignored what was gong on behind the scene. Consequently he continued to improve the investment recommendations from poor to satisfactory. But the author's real intention was to replace them after maximal 2½ years by top quality products requiring practical skills and professional knowledge. However, there was envy, greed, selfishness, and reform hostility like nowhere he had ever worked. This experience damaged his health, destroyed his banking career and future plans—condemned by the teaching of Buddhism, Confucianism, and Christianity.

In the following years of recession, the pressure to make a living forced him to work very hard with and without compensation. So for example to set up a global research program including investment strategies and macro- and micro- market reports with performance control for a rich and very demanding investor 1993-1994. Despite the good performance of his portfolio he was never happy as greed prevailed. One example was the author's recommendation of oil stock as he expected a rise of the share prices of about 30% in the next months.

"I want 100%" was his answer. Then he continued alone when the world's stock markets started the historically longest rally until the end of August 2000 illustrated by the development of the European and US share indexes: SMI from 1704 to 8000+, FTSE from 3106 to 6000+, DAX from 2015 to 6000+, CAC from 2096 to 3000+ and DJ from 3895 to 11000+. Thereafter, the author received financial statements to examine Slovakian companies for investments purposes, but the risks did not meet credit standards. But the analytical results were so accurate that a Slovakian manager wondered from where he received his information.

In September 1995, he was given a book with full of mathematical formulas by the Swiss Stock Exchange (SWX) to calculate the corporate actions. After analyzing and computerizing the figures, they were presented to the Index Commission, and since January 1, 1996, the SWX calculates and distributes the capital events as new products. Simultaneously, the author took part in the creation of the European DJ STOXX Indexes and wrote market reports for the SWX Annual Reports, from 1995 to 1999. As a free lancer he also taught the co-workers at TELEKURS AG, Zurich, cause, and influence of capital events on companies' equities and stock indexes. After all kinds of corporate actions of the SWX and DJ STOXX indexes have been calculated and stored, the downloading for new capital events has become routine work. Besides, its number reduced drastically because of the long lasting stock market crash due to the imploding internet bubble 2000-2003. Subsequently, a new challenge was the function as a CFO of a young high tech group encompassing five companies operating in five different countries to set up consolidated business and budget plans. But the weak stock market, coupled with a severe recession beginning in the fourth quarter of 2000, did dramatically dampen the business outlook.

Sometime later, when the manager of a pharmacy told the author about how people lived in Thailand, he asked himself, why live in Switzerland. A country where he made such bad experience, where deficiencies, and wrongdoings of managers are covered and uncovering is treason of internal matters, also gratitude is missing? After this revelation, he gave up and sold everything and booked the flight Zurich-Bangkok on July 6, 2003, one way only to Thailand. With hindsight, it was the best and fastest decision he have ever made to leave this country and to move to Thailand where Asian values—"to put the good of society above that of the individual"—is the concept by which they live.

Too much of good life makes people lazy,
paralyzes the economy and leads to divorce and suicide
In the splendid isolation of Switzerland, "the companies have become saturated and lazy" writes the Swiss consulting company Zehnder & Partner in the *TA* of September 30, 2004. And Jean-Pierre Roth, president of the Swiss National Bank, supports this statement since growth is only possible "when more can be produced in the working hours with new technologies".

> The slow growth of the Swiss economy was also again criticized by the OECD report published in the *NZZ* of January 6, 2006, recommending urgent measures such as to promote competition and innovation thus increasing productivity, to reduce barriers in the domestic market, to integrate woman and elderly people in the job market, and to have better control of the inflating public expenditures. Any failure of these fundamental structural reforms will result in a decrease of growth to 0.5% in 2025 aggravated by an increasing aging population to be supported by a decreasing number of younger people deteriorating the social security system of Switzerland.

But who of the well-off Swiss population cares what will happen in twenty years? Actually, many Swiss make more money than they really need. Subsequently, they can afford to work less, have more spare time, and enjoy a better life style. Past are the times of Ulrich Bremi, ex-entrepreneur and ex-member of the Swiss Parliament, who once stated, "We Swiss are better because we are in the workplace in the morning one hour earlier than all others". In fact, in the 1950s and 1960s the Swiss and the Germans were in Europe the most industrious people, striking rarely, compared to trade union members in Italy, France, and England.

Despite leading economically good lives, Switzerland has an above average divorce rate. In 2004, 18.000 marriages ended in divorce which was 6.8% more than in 2003 compared to 3.2% annually in the 1990s as recession prevailed. However, with divorce rates of 44% in 2004 and 45.5% in 2005 versus 15% in 1970, Switzerland is one of the worldwide "leaders in divorce". Another even more worrying statistic is the development of the committed suicides in this country being 2004 1.485, 2005 1.657 and 2006 1.467. Despite Switzerland wants desperately lower this rate the number of suicides increased sharply in 2007 to 1.800 or 20% respectively five victims each day according to the official Swiss police criminal statistic. The Swiss Federal Office for health (BAG) further informed that 10% of all Swiss tried to commit suicide once in the course of their life and between 15.000 to 25.000 people tried to end their life once in a year. Another sad record is that every second young person used a gun to end his life which is also more than in any other European country with the exception of Iceland.

The fact that Switzerland has in international comparison, exhibited an above-average high suicide rate leads to the assumption that this is the result of psychological disorders of which 25% of the Swiss people suffer but only 5% undergo an appropriate treatment. In fact in Switzerland the social climate is poisoned and the household incomes differ substantially of which 10% have an average annual income of only SFr 25.000. The richest 10% earn 10 times more while 146.000 people belong to the Working Poor. The top 2% have incomes of above SFr. 420.000 and the 300 richest people have increased their wealth by 40% in the last eight years according to the Swiss Revue of December 2008. No wonder that the most endangered groups of people are in the age of 18 to 25 years and elderly people over 74 years. Therefore suicide is the second highest cause of death of young people while in the elderly age group suicide it is the third largest reason of death. Thus the risks of young people suffering from psychological disorders without receiving appropriate support to become social burdens charging the economy and society billions are up to 10 times higher.

The above high rates of divorce, suicides and psychological disorders in a country enjoying for decades prosperity underline that many Swiss do not benefit from the good life. As the latter promotes envy, greed, and selfishness the beneficiaries enjoy their undemanding and overpaid jobs—particularly in the banking and insurance sectors, and they want it always to remain as such. And due to the legal protection of the status quo means reforms are missing and hindering stronger economy growth. Therefore people living comfortably in the business and private life are not aware of people suffering from psychological disorders being afraid to ask for help for many reasons. But the worldwide banking crises, the dramatically losses in the stock and real estate markets and the dismissal of many greedy and careless Swiss bankers 2007-2008 changed their comfortable life. Not used to a harder life style they turn to psychiatric clinics where the number of patients increased sharply while the number of suicides during this period was rising. Now they pay for receiving too much easy money for many years, copying others' work and not improving their professional knowledge and practical skills as only necessity is the mother of invention.

Contrary to the Swiss economy with its national Swissair Disaster 2001, the US economy developed much better and faster after the big bankruptcies of WORLDCOM, ENRON, and other corporate scandals in 2001. But the wrongdoers received prison sentences instead of golden parachutes. Not hindered by reform hostility, the Security Exchange Commission (SEC), the supervising body of the New York Stock Exchange (NYSE), set up laws and rules such as the Sarbanes-Oxley Act—detailed later in the chapter "The rise and Fall of Enron". These legal boundaries encourage freedom of expression in the workplace and protect critical employees or whistleblowers uncovering any wrongdoings. As a result of substantially improved working conditions, the USA became a knowledge economy encompassing all sectors of the industries and services. Driven by ideas, innovation and visions the US GDP growth rate was above 3.5% and the US productivity 3.1% in 2005 versus 1.7% respectively 1.6% in Switzerland. Not impressed by the short term cyclical recovery of the Swiss economy 2004/2006 and inflation rate of only 1%, the Swiss currency depreciated substantially against the EURO, the Chinese Yuan and other foreign currencies. In Thailand the depreciation of the SFr was 18% since November 2004 due to Thailand's average growth rate of 5% and remarkable foreign investments. The same is true of the small Eastern European country Slovakia where the SFr fell 21.5% against the Slovakian currency since 1996.

The following six chapters are quotations from excerpts of Swiss newspaper articles underlining the reality of everyday Swiss life.

1st Swiss economy in the purgatory
Quoted excerpts from the *NZZ* of November 10, 2002:

> Something is wrong in Switzerland—Strategic wrong decisions, entrepreneurial failures, and especially ethical and moral wrongdoings of managers and decision makers have undermined the confidence of the public and politic. A symbolic event bringing the Swiss economy and its elite downward was the beginning of the Swissair crises 2000/2001.

With some exceptions, such as Nestle and Novartis, many Swiss companies listed at the Swiss Stock Exchange (SMI) have changed or have been forced to change their CEOs and board members. In many cases, the reason was moral failure as good virtues went lost and knowledge was more highly esteemed than character. In the boom years of the 1990s, not the best qualified candidates were selected; instead brilliant pretenders showing off in the media by covering their deficiencies and wrongdoings due to Switzerland's underdeveloped understanding of checks and balances were chosen. The smallness of the country makes this understandable but prevents a rigorous exclusion of interest and personnel connections considered as Anglo-Saxon ideals.

After all these unpleasant events and scandals, the Swiss economy needs a Dante Purgatory, a process of personnel self-cleaning and a return to ethics and morals and a clear approach to managers with human values. In the selection process, not the physical appearance should prevail, but serious work and character. Besides, a framework has to be set up describing the most important rules and guidelines to prevent wrongdoings again. Of further importance is transparency for shareholders. Perhaps the Swiss economy will take the chance to make a new start.

2nd The crook in your own office
Quoted excerpts from the *NZZ* of August 10, 2005:

Switzerland is no longer a sound world. Ever since the Swissair collapse this observation has been regularly confirmed. As much as 73% of Swiss companies are affected by white-collar crime. The Federal Office for police estimates that white-collar crime in Switzerland weakens the gross domestic product annually up to 4%. In 2004, this would have amounted to over eight billion Swiss Francs. More than half of the white-collar crimes were perpetrated by co-workers of which 53% were senior managers and 32% middle managers. The crimes came to light because in 20% of the cases internal or external controls did not function and led to a further 20% of the cases coming to light through coincidence.

The discovery of criminal practices also occurs through cost controls, as well as by information from co-workers and external sources. Fraudulent activities are most frequent in bookkeeping or with false expense bills. A further investigation revealed that 35% of all Swiss employees it is acceptable to steal office materials from an employer illustrating how far the threshold for ethical and moral codes within the workplace has been stretched—criminal actions are no longer considered out of place. The fact that Switzerland has deficits because of bribery and corruption is clearly shown in past reports by the OECD and Transparency International.

3rd Who is afraid of whistleblowers?

Quoted excerpts from *TA* of August 5, 2005:

Whistleblowers are co-workers who uncovered fraud cases in companies. But for the Swiss Banking Association (SBV) whistleblowers are, above all, people poisoning the climate because names of colleagues and superiors would be dirtied by them and, therefore, would not be protected. This is just not the case says Daniel Jostisch, professor of the University of Zurich. The problem is that often it is not the individuals who are corrupt but the whole systems, including management, which would know how to protect itself. But according to Anna Schwoebel, Transparency International, the percentage of cases going undetected in Switzerland is almost 100% as whistleblowers mostly get punished or lose their jobs.

In contrast to Switzerland, in the USA, UK, New Zealand, Australia etc, whistleblowers are protected by law. The Swiss Banking Commission (EBK) wanted to implement these laws into the Swiss financial scene but was rebuffed by the syndicate representing the banks' interest. But in accordance with Schwoebel clear guidelines stating what is allowed and what is not have a positive effect. Jostisch's result is clear: cases of corruption can be uncovered only with whistleblowers. In the meantime the Swiss Government has also realized that whistleblowers uncovering criminal offences such as corruptions, fraud etc in the workplace must be protected. Therefore the department of justice has the intention to work out legal rules to motivate and to protect employees to uncover wrongdoings who lost their jobs in the past.

Therefore, one must protect them. In fact, only those are afraid who have to cover wrongdoings or their lack of skills and knowledge could be discovered.

4th My Lord, give us power for reforms
Quoted excerpts from the *Schweizer Revue* of July 2005:

> Switzerland is a high price country. For imported goods, we pay on average 20% more than Germany, and there is no reason for this because the strong Swiss franc reduces the prices of imports. Further weak points are the lack of integration into the European Union and the failed accomplishment of necessary reforms. By contrast, Austria increased the economy's output by 18% between 1996 and 2003, and the productivity rose by 18% versus 12% and 6% respectively in Switzerland. The country fears the future. Each adjustment to internationally valid rules is rejected. The system in Switzerland has become sluggish. In a country which has reached such a high standard of living one is more concerned with maintaining the status quo and keeping change out. Switzerland is not achievement-oriented and is content with 1% economic growth because the suffering pressure to achieve is missing in the Swiss workplace. It does not become a poorhouse but without reforms the way will slowly but surely, lead to there.

5th Swatch founder Nicolas G. Hayek:
Switzerland needs again entrepreneurs
Quoted excerpts from the *Schweizer Revue* of August 2005:

> The main shareholder and CEO of the Swiss International Group stated critically that many public speakers at universities and in the media have no feeling and no understanding for entrepreneurship. He further stated that they wrongly compare entrepreneurs with managers who only administer and take money and have no brilliant ideas and strategies. A good entrepreneur is like an artist who again creates something new and constantly makes new products.

The manager is frequently only an administrator without any clear strategy who does not want to risk his money and who tries to lead an enterprise according to the text book, and when it is a major failure he takes money anyway. What the country needs again are more entrepreneurs with passion, appropriate qualities, and 100% engagement for the profession as well as more R+D, education, innovation, and reformation to strengthen the Swiss workplace.

6th Destroying judgment for Switzerland

With the header "Economy Policy Reform, Going for Growth" the chief economist of the OECD, Jean Phillippe Otis, presented his study on March 1, 2005, in Paris and was published by the *NZZ* of March 1, 2005. The excerpts from the *NZZ* citing the above headline as conclusion are quoted as follow:

Otis pointed out that the gross domestic product per head for France, Germany, Italy, and Japan has fallen twenty-five to thirty percent under that of the USA. Switzerland, in particular, came off badly: This was surprising as it was one of the few countries which had, at the beginning of the 70s, a gross domestic product per head which was twenty-five percent higher than that of the USA. It has fallen without signs of stopping. It lost its lead, and, in fact, is now behind the USA more than fifteen percent. Otis fears even larger prosperity gaps in the future. As a result of this publication, the OECD politicians tried to help the situation by looking for ways to improve the standard of living. Each of the OECD countries is evaluated with comparable criteria, and already newly started reforms are described and recommended for those countries which have the most problems. Switzerland is one of those countries.

IV.
SWISS AND FOREIGN EDUCATION

Swiss Education

In 1976 and 1977, the author was asked by a German professor at the University of St Galle to give his students analyzing lessons including practical tests. Years later the professor told the author that for the former students working in the bank's credit- and research divisions the tests and the author's first book were very useful in their business. According to some sources, Switzerland's most important "commodity" is education along with Research and Development (R+D) which is crucial for the prosperity of the country. Thus, it wants the universities to be among the best worldwide.

However, to maintain and to improve the education standard universities depend also on the quality of its students. Therefore they are looking worldwide for the best talents. However, Swiss universities have no such choice as they must accept every candidate with a Swiss cantonal maturity diploma despite not having the qualifications needed to study at a Swiss university said rector A. Fischer of the University of Zurich in the *TA* of January 14, 2009. The reasons are insufficient language skills and lacking sufficient knowledge of math and statistics. Besides, they are unable to work independently, cannot work under pressure, are not used to criticism, are quickly discouraged and cannot understand scientific original text. In addition they have problems to plan and regulate their own independent learning. Due to unclear visions of their chosen discipline many new students do not know what is expecting them resulting to changes and lost semesters. Consequently Swiss universities are disadvantaged versus foreign universities which can select the best students also from abroad. Therefore it is difficult for Swiss universities to improve teaching standards to meet market requirements in a competitive environment. In fact, in many places of Asia, such as India, China, Japan, and Singapore, elite universities emerge. However, when finally students with deficiencies mentioned above become academicians they have by experience problems in the workplace. Instead that such graduates develop in the practice new ideas and know how they are de facto only expensive cars without wheels and useless. Worse Swiss graduates having the least theoretical and practical knowledge are the most arrogant ones. This is not surprising as a Swiss university degree is the ticket for the lift to reach quickly higher positions in the business life. On the other hand non-graduates must climb first the many steep stair cases to reach higher floors despite practical skills. In the meantime companies hiring graduates have become selective and check also the university degrees. This suits to the next chapter disclosing that the Swiss graduates of 2009 are seemingly not better than those of 2004.

Of the many Swiss universities only four of them are on the list of *The Times Education Supplement* classifying in 2005 the 200 best teaching schools worldwide. The four universities encompass two Federal Institute of Technology (FIT) in Zurich and Lausanne and two universities in Zurich and Geneva. The latter two appear for the first time on the list of elites. But what do the two FIT and the foreign universities make better? Both FIT schools have more educational freedom because the reporting line is only the Swiss Federation. Besides, both FIT and foreign universities select their foreign students before enrolling, thus reducing substantially costly dropouts. In the 1990s depending on the universities, they accounted for twenty-five percent to over forty percent off all students in their first year of study. Consequently, only bright, talented, and successful students maintain quality, brand, and prestige of a teaching body.

The good ranking of Zurich University is not surprising as its students are doing well also in the marketplace. The same is true for the Geneva University which is accredited for its good reputation in medical science. However, both universities and both Federal Institute of Technology have the same problems like other Swiss universities. These are the overcrowded lecture-halls hindering teaching and the very complicated and difficult educational supervising system. The latter was strongly criticized by an education expert of the independent *Think-Tank Swiss Avenir*, in his long report (in German) headed "Copy allowed Mr. Professor!" published in the *Swiss Weltwoche* of December 2005 of which the excerpts are quoted as follow:

The Swiss universities are mainly occupied with themselves. The seven cantonal or inter cantonal high schools with sixty part time education institutes, ten universities, and the two Federal Institute of Technology are administrated managed, and supported by a costly inflated red type. This creates more confusion and limits the autonomy and educational activities of the universities.

What is the reputation of many graduated Swiss in the market today?

Not better than in the past! Is the conclusion of an essay written by a CEO of Credit Suisse published in the Swiss *Weltwoche* of December, 2004, and quoted as follow: "The university teaching needs a quality offensive. A study place in Switzerland costs the taxpayer SFr 40.000 each year. Consequently, it would be the biggest social injustice, if a seemingly good university diploma cannot meet the quality requirements of the future employment". The Credit Suisse CEO was supported by the Swiss consulting company of Zehnder & Partner based on contracts with twenty-four CEOs of Swiss financial and industrial companies. Zender's statement was taken from excerpts published in the Tages Anzeiger of September 30, 2004, and quoted as follow: "Innovation is the Omega to survive: without risk there is no growth". But the Swiss have angst to fail, having the same thinking and little esteem for creativity. The education system is also to blame being good but lacking creativity. All Swiss students are taught to do the same thing and have the same concepts in their heads. The teachers go straight through an education plane, but creative thinking is missing from left to right. The consequences are that several CEOs do not hire anymore graduates from certain universities. The author too worked with such Swiss graduates. Lacking practical skills they were helpless in the workplace and copied others' work thus asking the question what did they learn at the university with the taxpayers' money? But the best coworkers were former bank apprentices with practical skills and good ideas thus being creative and productive.

However, not the students alone are to blame but also the teachers missing creative thinking. Consequently the challenge of the university body is to nominate professors not only with an extensive academician and theoretical background but also with a high "Emotional Quotient (EQ)" which is the emotional intelligence do determine the potential for learning the practical skills. They are based on its five elements: self-awareness, self-discipline, self-motivation, empathy and flexibility which are further explained in the chapter "Swiss Bank's Violation of Rules of Conduct & Ethics 1989-2003". By teaching "EQ" future managers will accept more criticism. Presently all have same school, same viewpoint, and whoever thinks differently is a bad student. What makes the difference of American and China teaching? They did abandon recitation in favor of classroom interaction that encourages students to think independently a means to stimulate economy growth according to Newsweek of August 28, 2006.

Research from the Swiss universities too is not highly demanded in the market place. In 2004 the Swiss companies spent SFr 4.046 MLN for outsourced R+D. From this amount more than half was paid abroad, about SFr 1.000 MLN to Swiss enterprises and only SFr 259 MLN to Swiss universities. This is in contrast to the American universities generating substantial income from R+D as they are more practically oriented and entrepreneurial. Result: due to long established links between academia and industry, American universities earn more than one billion dollars a year alone from royalties and license fees. Additionally more than 170 universities have "business incubators" of some sort, and dozens have their own venture funds. However, in the Swiss economy a certain functionalism prevails—it administers instead of innovating improvements. The same is true in the politic according to excerpts from the NZZ of June 29, 2006, quoted as follow:

> "In Switzerland govern means good and circumspect administrate without strategic target. Instead to make a pragmatically policy the government follows a shortsighted little step policy of interest which hinders to realize big long term targets and big projects". This statement is also in line with a speech of the president of the Swiss people party at a meeting of August 19, 2006, in the Swiss town Baar complaining "that too much red tape is dominating the public administrations acting slow and highhanded. Therefore they should be cleaned up".

Today, in Switzerland and abroad, companies give preference to graduates with practical skills who have increased their knowledge through learning in the workplace—thus achieving the best results. Consequently, Swiss universities not providing practical teaching and business ethics as they do in the USA, hinder graduates' performance within the marketplace. On the other hand, an improvement in the quality of teaching cannot be achieved with too many students paying too little. Therefore, the big attraction of the Swiss universities is not the quality per se but instead the low annual tuition fee of SFr 1.400 for Swiss and SFr 1.600 for foreigners. Furthermore, 75% of the foreign students study in Switzerland not because of the university but firstly because of the attractive city of Zurich and of the country according to the NZZ of December 12, 2006. However, without substantial higher tuition fees of about a quarter or half of SFr 40.000 the Swiss universities cannot upgrade teaching quality for a growing number of students hardly finding a place in the lecture-halls.

Besides, the rapid rising costs of higher education can no longer be borne by the taxpayers alone. Particularly as the beneficiaries of higher education at low costs earn substantially more than their fellow citizens whose taxes subside their tuition fees. Aware of these facts and in line with the US universities the European governments are starting to recognize that is no longer feasible to pre finance with general taxes the soaring expenses of constantly more future high income graduates who have yet to learn the practical skills.

Nevertheless, bright and talented students avoid cheap universities and choose schools with worldwide brand names as best referenced in the market. Thus, they are willing to pay much higher tuition rates. The small student contribution in Switzerland is also confirmed that only fifteen percent of the university costs are carried by students and third parties compared to around over fifty percent at Harvard (USA) and around fifty percent at Princeton (USA). But true is also that the Federal Government spends over $100 billion a year on student aid, and elite universities make every effort to subsidy poorer students. Finally, and most important, is the fact that today fifty percent of the managers of Swiss companies listed on the SMI Blue Chip index of the Swiss Stock Exchange are foreigners. Well know examples are ABB with a German CEO, Credit Suisse Group with an American CEO and Nestle with an English CEO on the top. Besides, the share of managers with university degrees is only twenty-five percent in Switzerland as they start as bank employees, commercial clerks, and bookkeepers and work their way up to management through the company.

English education
Britain's six elite colleges Oxford University (founded in 1096), Cambridge University (founded in 1209), London School of Economics, University of Edinburgh, University of St Andrews and Imperial College London have an excellent reputation in the world of education. Many successful graduates became later VIP in science, economy and politics. However, based on excerpts of Stanly Reed's detailed report in the Business Week of December 5, 2005, he stated that even the University of Oxford has problems as quoted as follow:

> There are shortfalls not enough firepower to compete with US rivals, infrastructure badly in need of repair, current decision-making bodies unwieldy and lacking independence, access to the university is still class-bound and narrow, and professors see themselves as above accountability.

But Oxford is willing to solve its problems to turn into an internationally famous research leader across the board and recruit not only the best British students and faculty but also the crème de la crème of the world—even if that means cutting the number of the Britons.

Nevertheless, "an increasing number of US students discover Britain's universities because they are much cheaper compared to US universities. Besides, their graduates are also welcomed by US employers such as Goldman Sachs, Morgan Stanley and Pentagon" writes Mark Scott in his essay "Who Needs Harvard or Yale?" in the Business Week of September 25, 2006. In fact, of the six British elite colleges the University of St. Andrews has the lowest annual tuition costs with $20.034 while the University of Oxford is the most expensive one with $27.839 but a bargain compared to US universities with annual average tuition costs of $33.774. No wonder that 2.201 US students—a fourfold increase since 1996—applied in 2005 at British universities but only 948 were accepted by Britain's Universities & Colleges Admissions Service (UCAS). But studying in England seems to be harder as class hours are kept to a minimum, normally less than ten hours per week. During the rest of the time the students must take part in small seminars and larger lectures. No homework is required as independent study is the rule. But in order to succeed self-discipline, self-motivation and self-education are needed rather than rely on professors. Social life too at British universities is different from US universities with a wide range of sport, campus and cultural activities. As a consequence of studying harder but at lower costs and by making a different culture experience the US students in Britain may have more pains but may have more gains than their American counterparts.

US Education
In 1982, shortly after joining the Swiss branch of a major U.S. the author was sent to the US headquarters in New York to attend a six-month credit and test seminar to learn the new business strategy. Of special interest was the practical teaching and thinking of instructors and graduates from the US universities. Despite the fact that the author got maximum marks in the case studies, there was no envy from US graduates. As a consequence, his stay was cut short after three months, disappointing him terribly to go back to Switzerland. In the Swiss branch, he was then rewarded and promoted until its closure in 1986 due to the cut-throat competition in the European credit business.

Nevertheless, it was the best experience in the performance oriented major U.S. where good work was appreciated as documented by the selected following summarized examples:

Date: February 14, 1983: From World Banking Group (WBG) Credit Training, New York, to the Lending Officer Candidate. Re: Performance of Martin Zumbuehl in the round of Individual Cases ending October, 1982, in New York: "Martin did an outstanding job in Individual Cases. Even though his time in New York was cut short, he was able to fully complete five of the eight cases. His analyses demonstrated a very sound and thorough knowledge of credit. By the end, Martin was able to complement his strong credit skills with a refined and polished written presentation adhering to the general format and structure used in New York. He was very open to constructive criticism and was an active participant in the program, He even took it upon himself to assist other participants in understanding the specifics of credit which was of benefit to all and it was a real pleasure to have Martin in the program – "Overall Outstanding".

Date February 20, 1985: From the Commodities Group, New York, to the corporate heads of Zurich/Geneva US Branches. Re: Speedy approval of Martin Zumbuehl's credit recommendation: "This credit package was recently approved. I wanted to drop a note regarding this analysis. What struck me most about the analysis was the way it came straight to the point and did not avoid any of the important issues. I personally thought this was most refreshing, and as a result, contrary to some analyst' misconceptions, it procured a speedy approval".

The practical way of US teaching results from the forging links between academics and industry. Thus the US universities are more than ivory towers which have also established a counterbalance to the power of the faculty in the person of a president. This allows some of them to act more like entrepreneurial firms than lethargic bodies according to the *Economist Survey Higher education* of September 10, 2005. Therefore, the success of US higher education is not just money; it is the result of organization confirmed by the ranking list of the world's top ten—which are eight American universities plus Oxford and Cambridge—established by the Jiao Tong University, Shanghai. This 2006 ranking list is based on a mixture of indications such as research, performance incl. Nobel prices and articles. Clearly the best of all is the Harvard University (USA) established 1636—teaching 20.000 students with annual expenses of $2.8 BLN and an endowment of presently $26 BLN thus the world's richest university—followed by the seven other US universities which are Stamford University, CALIF-Yale University, CONN-California Institute of Technology, CALIF-University of California, Berkeley, CALIF-Massachusetts Institute of Technology, MASS-University of California, CALIF-Columbia University, NY. Within the world's top thirty universities, twenty-three are based in the United States, four in Britain, two in Japan and one in Switzerland - the Federal Institute of Technology, thus reflecting the size and strength of the countries they represent. The United States have technologies and service of the highest standards and a large industrious population. Logically, they have also a big potential in bright individuals as students and graduates creating outstanding achievements in the praxis. No wonder that the US universities employ currently seventy percent of the Nobel-prize winners, producing about thirty percent of the world's output of articles on science and engineering, and forty-four percent of the most frequently cited articles. Nevertheless, Jeffrey E. Garten, former dean of the Yale School of Management, wrote a critical essay "B-Schools: Only a C+ in Ethics" published in the *Business Week* of September 5, 2005, of which following quoted excerpts are of interest:

> American B-schools cannot turn someone who is dishonest into a virtuous person nor can a MBA program give sometimes the backbone to make a moral decision that risks the loss of a company. What business schools can do, however, is teach students how to apply value judgments when issues are not black and white. An obvious place to start, the admission process: In evaluating applications, business schools should ask prospective students pointed questions in their essays and interviews about ethical turning points in their lives. Admission officials should also plumb views about current moral controversies in the business world. When soliciting references, business schools should specifically request input on a candidate's character. The answers to all these questions should be evaluated with the same seriousness as grades and test scores. In addition new courses should be added beyond what is normally required. All students should gain a fundamental understanding of business law and most prestigious faculty should lead the way in promoting ethics, or students will quickly infer the subject is not critical.

As a condition for tenure, the faculty should be required to pass a rigorous exam on such matters, graded by experts inside and outside the academy.

Results: US professors are teaching successfully in their disciplines but most had little training in teaching ethics and morals. Consequently, the markets criticized the US universities for not being a stronger bulwark to prevent corporate scandals and to avoid poor business ethics. Besides, it is no longer a must for young corporate up-and-comers to apply to B-schools after four years on the job. Now managers are promoting some talents without degrees. Goldman Sachs & Co finds those people increasingly to be the norm rather than the exception. Goldman and others provide a growing array of management education chipping away at the traditional MBA. Over the past five years, many well known companies that had previously heavily recruited MBAs have altered their hiring mix. Large consulting firms such as McKinsey & Co had downsized the percentage of new MBA hires and added more students and industry professionals. The shift is fundamental not cyclical—hiring non-MBAs has become for companies more comfortable. MBA schools must find ways to break through recruiters' feelings that even top tier MBAs are becoming a commodity.

Regardless of the above criticism the US universities with brand names still attract bright and talented students who are also granted government support if needed. Additionally, elite universities make every effort to subsidize talented poor students. In fact in America higher education has long been considered not as a privilege but as a right. The 1862 passage of the Land-Grant College Act brought education to people by establishing universities in every state to provide training in all kind of professions. In other countries this right depends on economical, social and political conditions. In Switzerland for example studying at the universities seems to be a class-bound privilege documented by a study of the Swiss Federal Office of Statistics in December 2006. The latter disclosed that only 16% of the Swiss students come from the lower social class, 25% from the middle class, 28% from the higher middle class and 31% from the high society.

Conclusion of Swiss and Foreign Education

The challenge of Swiss, British, US and Asian top universities is to teach students what the markets require. This is difficult for the Swiss universities which cannot select and enroll the best students. Besides, as there are too many students paying too low a tuition the quality of teaching and student bodies suffer accordingly as the teacher's time is limited to take more care of students, to do research, and to handle too much paperwork. Besides, Swiss universities share the same problems with the American universities in respect of lacking teaching ethics and morals and the markets hiring increasingly industry professionals. The English and US top universities with fewer students are better off despite decreased money inflow and increased competition from the market. But having learned from the aforementioned criticism, they have the capacity and will to meet these challenges and competitively attract bright and talented students from anywhere. The *Economist Survey* sees as the most significant development in higher education the emergence of a super-league of global universities which regards the whole world as their stage. The United States have almost a monopoly on the world's best universities providing also access to higher education for the bulk of those who deserve it. In the light of the above, it is no surprise that the winners of the Nobel Prize in economic science in 2006 and 2008 were both from the United States!

V.
SWISS AND FOREIGN FINANCE

Swiss finance

"The Swiss financial place should be a world leader also in research and teaching" was the conviction of the president of the Swiss Banking association (SBV) supported by Swiss bankers and Swiss universities published in the *NZZ* of August 20, 2005. However, in the light of the 2007-2008 World's banking disaster damaging particularly the Swiss financial place financially, ethically and morally the president's plans have become dreams. Therefore they were mentioned only for entertainment purposes. So he wanted that the small world of Swiss finance, with 320 domestic banks encompassing cantonal-, regional-, local- and private banks and the headquarters of UBS and Credit Suisse employing a staff of around 120.000, should lead and teach the vast sophisticated world of finance. As a result, a new Swiss Finance Institute (SFI) was founded in the French speaking city of Lausanne starting the activities on January 1, 2006. The purpose of the SFI is to offer sustained strength to Swiss universities in research as well as education and training in the areas of banking and finance. It has been of central importance to win the support of the leading universities of Switzerland for the common good outlined the president. He further dreamed that the SFI should have a leading position of Switzerland within Europe in areas of banking and risk management etc.

Not a dream is that with the SFI and the Institute of Management Development (IMD) two independent business schools are operating in the same small French speaking Swiss city of Lausanne. Asking questions why this newly founded and unknown SFI is not incorporated as a Swiss banking faculty in the IMD? Thus, using their infrastructure and creating synergies, and saving money! The IMD is the world's leading business school with good international rankings, teaching market needs and values, is not operating with public money and gets more applicants than it can accept.

The SFI project should leverage SFr 200 million from promotions and research. The annual costs of SFr 18 million partially financed also by public money are an additional burden for tax payers. The latter support already substantially with SFr 5.4 BLN annually the expenditure of the Swiss universities. Of this sum, the Swiss Confederation and Swiss Cantons gave eighty-five percent while students and third parties provided fifteen percent. An exception is the university St. Galle which received fifty-five percent of its income from tax payers and forty-five percent from other sources. Nevertheless, the Swiss financial place is behind Anglo-Saxon countries for years in the fields of mathematics, macro and micro economics, risk management, financial analysis etc. this is not surprising as many Swiss banks cultivated the standstill, encouraging a   lack of creativity, low productivity, and reform hostility.

The above is confirmed by a study of the Basic Economics AG BAK of November 2, 2004, demonstrating "that Swiss bank employees have become substantially less productive since the middle of the 1990s in comparison to their colleagues in New York, Boston, Brussels, Frankfort, and Vienna". The latter is one of the many reasons why the Swiss financial place lost ground versus London, New York, Frankfort, and Brussels in the last 10 years. Still worse as new cash for investments is increasingly generated and managed in London, Frankfort, New York, Dubai, Singapore, and Hong Kong, the Swiss financial place with its many small and medium-sized banks operating mainly nationally cannot compete with the above foreign financial places. Last but not least due to the World's banking crises many weaknesses of the Swiss banks came to surface and customers lost their confidence.

In the appendix under chapter "Wishful Thinking – Swiss Financial Place should join World's Champions- League" the author questions again the president's dreams. Nevertheless, in the Swiss security business, average salaries are in the range of SFr 200.000 to 300.000 although their work is hardly worth the cost. And who are the grossly overpaid employees? Mostly financial analysts and middle managers financially not responsible versus customers losing substantially for administrating portfolios, supervising securities, structured products or derivatives, tracking share- and bond markets, tinkering with profit estimations, and writing mostly easy purchase but seldom difficult sales recommendations for fearing of angry customer reactions. Besides, as the   markets   create   the   increase/decrease   in   value   creative achievements are not really necessary.

This is different in case of structured products or derivatives based on underlying shares and bonds. Used for hedging and all kind of portfolio strategies they are particularly appreciated in volatile markets and thus generating higher earnings. Therefore the market for such derivatives reached in Switzerland alone triple digit billions of SFr. in the last years. As a consequence and to save time and money the many lengthy und often flattering and misleading research recommendations are better used to fill the waste bins. This statement was already confirmed 1991 by the Extel Survey, London, in an appropriate article which has nothing lost of its actuality:

> "There is an old adage that in a bull market who needs research and in bear market who cares! But every day research piles up on the investment managers' desk. As a result three out of five managers are likely to throw three quarters of that early morning pile straight in the waste bin. Compounded by all the research output from the City that could mean 30-40 tons of papers are shipped each week to the managers. But how much is really needed? Quantity has very often accounted more than quality because the material was treated as part of public relation exercise and the research department as unavoidable overhead".

The following examples reading partly like jokes are selected from many anecdotes which document how the investment "research recommendations" were often wrong, misleading and even cheating investors. They were produced by bank financial analysts often without ethics and morals, missing practical skills and professional knowledge. Driven by greed, arrogance and ego they were also speculating with the customers' investments.

EXAMPLE 1
Losses from wrong research recommendations of Swiss analysts
The Swiss company, Interdiscount, was a very successful retailer of consumer electronics. After the unification of East and West Germany, 1990 sales were soaring and share prices went up. At the price of SFr 3150 in March 1991, a young financial analyst with a Swiss University degree wrote a buy recommendation. But it was a sell due to the following reason: 1. End of the purchasing boom in East Germany. 2. In the red-hot Swiss real estate market the company's fixed assets were pushed up with borrowed capital. 3. Sales were decreasing and some consolidated companies were changed without explanation. Alerted to these facts, the writer of the study remarked arrogantly:

"You are just jealous for not being a young Swiss academician", and the "chef analyst" also with a Swiss university degree supported him strongly while the author was attacked and libeled for "not being cooperative". Finally, the shares in question were strongly recommended to advisers and clients anyway. Shortly later, the interest rates soared to record highs, the real estate market collapsed, and the share prices plummeted. But in March 1994, the same Swiss academicians recommended the shares again at the price of SFr 2500 mentioning that the "price is right as the company is doing well". The market was better informed and in 1996, the company went bankrupt. And the shares were de listed at the price of SFr 7.50. Customers and investment advisers lost substantially. But who cared about? No one!

EXAMPLE 2
Innocent and misleading 100 page investment report
In August 2000, another financial analyst with a Swiss University degree and head of Swiss research recommended strongly to buy shares of Mövenpick, an international Swiss restaurant and hotel chain, at SFr 795 with target price of SFr 1300 in the coming months. But the one-hundred page study absorbed too much time and was finally worthless as things changed. The cited new, strong, leading team of Mövenpick was not complete anymore, and the problems of the company were simply ignored. The market punished the writer and pushed the share price down to SFr 410 in September 2002. Still worse as from 2000 to 2005, the company could not generate any operating net income. The share price plummeted further to SFr 282.50 at the end of December 2005. In the meantime the controlling shareholders decided to go private. As a result the shares were delisted in December 2006 and mislead customers and investment advisers carried the loss.

EXAMPLE 3
Fatal theoretical assumptions of the CIO ignoring market facts
At the beginning of 1990 a Swiss graduate and chief investment officer demonstrated with designed tables that Swiss inflation and interest rates would sink at the end of 1990 and 1991. However, the converse was true as the employees were fully compensated for the inflation losses, and car imports increased anyway—even at higher prices. However, the false assumptions led to a wrong investment strategy of the bank for the years from 1990 to 1991. But in 1992, unemployment increased dramatically. Imports of cars dropped, and the stop to pay further inflation compensation resulted in lower inflation and interest rates.

EXAMPLE 4
Launching of a Japan equity basket being a flop from the start

What are economic models? Often, they are wrong assumptions illustrated by the development of the Japanese stocks in 1999 lagging far behind the booming European and US stock markets. In the belief that the Japanese shares were under-priced, the CIO created in the second half of 1999 a Japan basket while the Nikkei index was 22.000 points at that time. However, he was not aware that mostly foreigners bought and pushed up the Japanese stock as Japan's big structural economic problems remained unsolved. The awakening was bitter as in October 2002 the Nikkei Index dropped to 8.400. Due to improved capitalization of the banks, weaker Yen and stronger US economy the Nikkei index reached 16.000 at the end of 2005. Therefore optimistic experts forecasted index figures of 17.000 and 19.000 for 2006 and 2007 respectively. However, with the beginning of the world's financial crises 2007, strong Yen, weak US economy and new recession in Japan the Nikkei Index plummeted below 7.000 points in November 2008 with no recovery in sight to reach ever 22.000 points once again.

EXAMPLE 5
Cheating investors by providing false information

With the blow up of the internet balloon at the end of the 1990s many fraudulent activities of US financial analysts came to surface. Such a case was telecom analyst Grubman selling 1998-2000 all kind of shares and bonds to customers amounting to $53 BLN. Still in 2001 he confirmed his "Strong buy" recommendation of WORLDWCOM as "it has the best assets of the whole telecom industry". Worse he downgraded WORLDWCOM only after the company has already missed the profit targets by 50%. The market reaction was dramatically because the company's shares and bonds lost so much of its value that they became worthless and were de listed. Nevertheless he received a golden parachute of $35 MLN despite the court blamed him with following words: "We have here an independent analyst who is neither independent and apparently cannot analyze". Other practices were selling to customers stock which was bank internal junk.

EXAMPLE 6
Creative bookkeeping to show off better results

However, not only analysts but also companies lost business ethics to show off better results. IBM for example improved the 4th quarter result 2001 by creative bookkeeping. Subsequently the markets worldwide reacted sour after disclosing that this was not the only case in the practice.

IBM used the proceeds of the sale of a business unity of $290 MLN to reduce the operating costs. This was legally correct but it provided a wrong picture of the operating profit. Other companies created provisions in good years in order to be used for a price reduction for a takeover of a company later.

EXAMPLE 7
Economist and Financial Analyst?

After finishing his economy study at a Swiss university he started working at a big Swiss bank as a financial analyst for 20 years. Thereafter followed job no 2 in an auditing and investment company where he had problems with his manager. Being always friendly the author liked to support him. His university degree and good references helped him to find quickly job no 3 in a private bank where the manager was again the problem. Hearing that 1993 the author was hindered to occupy a lucrative bank position the economist took the opportunity to get this job no 4. There he should write a bank report but failed to do it. So he called the author and some days later he had finished the report in question but no thanks. Asking the economist of the where about he sent the author a French version but it was a plagiarism. Lucky again he got job no 5 as an economy redactor of a financial newspaper to write a report of a large battered Swiss company. The author was also charged with this task but was not informed that the economist got the same job as well. The author stated which measures have to be taken to overcome the crisis but was not published. The economist stated that the company will be soon bankrupt due to the short term debt of SFr 19 BLN but ignored completely the current assets of SFr 22 BLN thus missing basic knowledge. The editor in chief offered his apologies to the company. As a result followed job no 6 as a "financial and ethic analyst" with a well known asset manager where he is also not anymore.

EXAMPLE 8
Insurance and Top Analyst?

Confucius was not a friend of pretenders. Therefore he would have also disliked the "insurance analyst" with a Swiss University degree taking over the author's construction work including banks and insurance companies. And as the "insurance analyst" benefited substantially of the author's work and teaching he cultivated close contacts also with the media. Subsequently he was called „expert", "top analyst", "insurance analyst" etc. But the realty was different. So one day a customer called the "insurance analyst" and asked him for details of the composition of an insurance company's equity.

But unable to answer this question he called the author who was first hesitating. "Please help me and do it for me" sounded it helplessly on the other end of the line. The author insisted to talk with the customer directly and informed him "Unfortunately no one in this bank can give you this information so please call Swiss Private Bank Bear and contact analyst XY". The customer was very grateful.

EXAMPLE 9
Arrogance?

One day a redactor of the newspaper AGEFI called the "chef analyst" with Swiss University degree asking him some little questions. At the end the "chef analyst" wanted to know from the redactor: "Is my name mentioned in the newspaper?" After a little pause the "chef analyst" added: "It is the wish of the top management that published interviews must always bear the name of the informant". This was not true and AGEFI published the other day a large bold header of 1½ cm reading "INTERVIEW WITH THE "CHEF ANALYST" and below in small letters some text.

1937-2001 Rise and Fall of SWISSAIR

What is a holy cow? It is an Indian animal living everywhere without control, untouchable, and protected from slaughtering by law. The same was true of Swissair operating without control everywhere, untouchable to criticism and too precious to fall. In fact, Swissair was Switzerland's label, a national symbol, the country's flagship, and the pride of the Swiss. But they were not aware that with the end of the regulated air traffic, this high cost airline became a money loser lacking competitiveness. Instead, to restore profitability, the blinded management created the hunter strategy to grab market shares with ailing foreign airlines bought at high cost with borrowed capital to become Europe's fourth largest airway group. These facts, the cut-throat competition and the poor cash management let to the grounding of all Swissair planes worldwide on October 2, 2001, and to the following bankruptcy of the company. By comparing this national disaster with a small country of only 41.285 square km versus the USA with 9.376.623 square km and national economies of estimated $372 billion respectively $13.153 billion in 2006 the Swissair collapse was a much bigger failure than that of the US companies Enron and WORLDCOM in which the wrongdoers received long term prison sentences from the US Court.

The bankruptcy of Swissair became a court case and the overcharged district court of Bûlach/Zurich needed five years to investigate. During this time the court established a bill of indictment of over one hundred pages to accuse the nineteen managers and board members. The charges were based on more than 4.150 big standard files and electronic materials encompassing 750 entertainment films. What the judge particularly accused in his revised bills of indictment of July 13, 2006 was mismanagement—no mentioning of the deterioration of the financial situation especially after the terror attacks in New York on 9/11/2001—and the missing embedment of the entrepreneurial decisions in the economically environment at that time. The court trial lasted from January 2007 until July 2007. Based on the long agenda of accusations everyone expected justice. Consequently appropriate big was the disappointment of all Swiss that the 19 accused were acquitted by the Swiss court as misconduct and the bankruptcy of Swissair was not a criminal act despite ethically and morally not acceptable.

Buyers and customers trusting the banks' stock recommendations often lost substantially, but no one cared about the wrong investment decisions which are legally market risks. Worse in the above Swiss cases was that warnings were arrogantly ignored thus acting against the interests of customers and investment consultants of the bank—but the Swiss graduates were promoted anyway. In the case of Swissair, with prominent board members also from Swiss banking circles, no graduate financial analyst dared to recommend Swissair stock for "sell" even though the company was and had been, a "lame duck" long time before the grounding. This illustrates also how university degrees formerly were the key for good jobs in Switzerland without practical experience and skills. Consequently, only "buy" reports were produced and "supported" by the upward trend of the Swiss Stock market starting with a SMI index figure of 1000 on June 1, 1987, soaring to 8489 on July 21, 1998. Dropping only temporarily during the Asian crisis 1997/1998 and rising up again thanks to the boom of the new economy. Consequently there were almost no market risks and no analytical skills were needed. But during the worldwide crash of the stock markets from September 2000 until summer 2002, the high tech shares of the new economy suffered most. Worse was the unethical behavior of innocent and fraudulent analysts, offering stocks of troubled and bankrupt companies. Result: Thousands of investors lost billions of US dollars in Europe and USA as many of these offered shares failed to recover after 2003 when the worldwide stock markets rebounded again.

In which bank division Swiss employees make the most money?
In the fund business where fund managers are often failed financial analysts who administer more than 5.000 fund products with a volume of around SFr 600 billion of which many differ only by names! What do they do? They copy mainly an index by buying and selling shares depending upon market fluctuations like a trader of fruit and vegetables. But fund administrators are far better off by cashing up to CHF 500.000 p.a. being part of the annual fees round 1.5% plus other expenses of round 0.5% to 1.0%. Thus reducing performance and yields accordingly of bonds and shares although they beat seldom the index. Examples are the managed Swiss Small Stock funds which are often not traded and cannot be sold if necessary due to the small size and lack of liquidity giving a wrong picture of the performance and subsequently are misleading small investors.

What is the much better and cheaper alternative? Exchange Traded Fund (EFT)! They function like managed funds but with multiple advantages such as realizable at any time, lower costs, transparency, showing daily volume, real time computation, tax benefits and ETFs must not be sold for liquidity reasons. What are the international markets saying? For example the Swiss Small Stock ETF of Credit Suisse performed in line with the appropriate index but plus dividends four times per year. On March 31, 2006, the worldwide 500 listed ETF at 33 stock exchanges have reached a volume of $456.5 BLN according to Morgan Stanley Research. The USA are the largest ETF market with 216 funds and a volume of $330.4 BLN followed by Europe with 196 funds and a volume of $64.6 BLN while the share of Japan was only $33 billion. The strong worldwide ETF-growth will continue as 170 new funds are in planning. At the Swiss Stock Exchange (SWX), the number of ETFs will be 70 at the end of 2006 compared to 34 in 2005.

Result: in the USA the formerly lucrative managed fund business has lost its luster for investors as well as for the large financial institutions due to strong competition, conflict of interest, and thin profit margins. Therefore, Citigroup, Merrill Lynch, and others sold their managed fund business. Not so in Switzerland where administrated and managed funds are still a lucrative business for a relatively small number of bank related issuers of fund products due to upheld high fees and expenses. Therefore private and institutional investors administrating hundreds of billions of Swiss francs of employees' saving invested in managed fund products should sell or to switch it into ETFs similar to the Americans.

Thus the financial assets of millions of hard working employees would not only performing and yielding much better, the risks of wrongdoings by managers of 8000 Swiss pension funds are limited. In fact, the recent Swiss private banking and pension scandal was rising questions also by a member of the Board of Directors of the Swiss National Bank whether "all these thousands of pension funds can be properly managed and supervised?" published the *Tages Anzeiger* of September 13, 2006. Besides, the wrongdoings by Swiss pension and bank managers misusing employees' savings for making personally undisclosed huge profits provoked also criticism countrywide. Now people have enough and want better rules in the Swiss financial place to prevent future violations of ethics and morals.

2007-2008 The new banking crises driven by greed & derivatives triggering off the world's biggest financial disaster

With the end of the internet bubble 2000 and after the bankruptcy of the two largest US companies ENRON and WORLDCOM 2001 tougher rules like the Sarbanes-Oxley Act were enforced. Thus the world's share markets were cleaned up from the scandals and wrongdoings. However, the gradually decrease of the interest rates from six percent to low as one percent generated abundant liquidity. This blessing was the start of a new boom in the real estate and mortgage markets which collapsed formerly in the USA in the 1980s, in Switzerland and in Japan in the 1990s. But contrary to the present world's financial disaster practically no derivatives were used or misused. The soaring real estates prices attracted also many speculators including big banks taking advantage of the cheap capital costs. Subsequently mortgages were granted to future home owners who were in the past not creditworthy. But as long as the relationships between lenders and borrowers were limited to single transactions the credit business was under control. But with the new form of financing called securitization the formerly single mortgage loans were bundled to new products called "Asset Backed Securities" (ABS) or "Mortgage Backed Securities" (MBS) and sold as interest bearing bonds yielding much higher and enabling the banks to discharge or clean their balance sheets. However, the discovery that part of the sub prime ABS/MBS were fraudulently labeled as prime the market lost its confidence.

Starting modestly in the 1980s these financial vehicles or derivatives developed to a multi trillion Dollar business. But as greed and fraud was also with of the party millions of MBS rated as first grad contained also sub prime or junk to achieve much higher interest income.

It was also greed when careless sub prime lenders offered mortgages to people who could hardly afford to pay their debts often at high interest rates. The default of such loans did not worry the lenders as they simply repossessed the property and tried to make a profit of the sale. This looked like a win-win deal for the dealers but proved years later to be short sighted as the deterioration of the real estate market made the real estates cheaper than the outstanding mortgage loans and the MBS derivates. Besides, the fact that the MBS increased from $1.500 BLN 1998 to $4.000 BLN 2003 the MBS market went slowly out of control and making it increasingly risky. Therefore the launching of the hottest credit derivative products being synthetic collateralized debt obligations (CDO) based on the risky MBS market was a casino like speculation. Worth still was the continued large production of highly sophisticated derivatives avoided by the markets. Thus the banks were unable to evaluate their structured products being used to pump up the credit volumes multiple times. Therefore only hot air was produced with the effect that the new bubble imploded like those in the past. As a result the banks in the USA lost $648 BLN, in Europe $288 BLN and elsewhere $27 BLN according to Bloomberg in November 2008 resulting in the world's biggest financial disaster 2007-2008.

For further reference the author mentioned in the preface "What is the purpose of the appendix"? An article of the Business Week of May 23, 2005, warning of the coming disaster with the header: "Taking Risk to Extremes – the serving of the huge wave in global credit market was so far successful etc". However, two years later this huge wave became a powerful Tsunami badly damaging the world's financial markets including the assumingly waterproof risk models hitting terribly the biggest Swiss bank UBS which was safeguarded by the Swiss Government 2008.

English Finance
Who are the rich customers of the Swiss London offshore banks? Also rich Russians living in London! In the lengthy report "Welcome to Londongrad" and published in the magazine *Forbes Global* of May 23, 2005, Michael Freedman published interesting information why the Russians love London. The following quoted excerpts also demonstrate the growing importance of London as the world's second largest financial place.

> With big wallets and bigger dreams, Russia's elite are making the British capital their home.

After seventy years of communism and twenty years of gangster capitalism, approximately 250.000 Russians from the former Soviet Union now live in London. Countless more have property or a financial presence there.

Many are seeking Western partners for investments – Western lawyers, investment advisers, and public relation agents. They have injected millions of pounds of sterling into the UK economy, buying houses and luxury goods. But of Russians' special interests are the strong capital markets and the favorable tax laws. Besides, Moscow has not a judicial system like Britain's that protects them from unwelcome inquisitions. By 2004, forty percent of the nation's $546 billion economy was controlled by twenty-two business groups, according to Moscow investment firm, Hermitage Capital Management. Money flowed out as fast as the millionaires. Between 1998 and 2004, $102 billion capital left Russia. Much of it went to offshore accounts in Switzerland and elsewhere.

From there it is impossible to trace, but tax lawyers say that UK offers unique tax advantages to people with assets offshore. Most countries require their residents, foreigners included, to pay taxes on worldwide income and capital gains. "But UK residents can set up their offshore accounts in such a way as to legally avoid these taxes", says Joel Mc Donald, a lawyer at the law firm Salans Salons in London. Thus a Russian billionaire can hold stock offshore, sell and use the proceeds to buy a London mansion—all without paying taxes on the gain. The UK government has considered closing the loophole, but it pulled back. That would mean killing the property market to say nothing of denting the pay of international lawyers and accountants as it's quite a great industry for a UK tax adviser", says Joel Mc Donald.

Although some oligarchs may be politically exposed, most of the 250.000 Russians are mainly wealthy people. Subsequently the latter, the London Stock Exchange (LSE), and the Russian treasury benefit directly and indirectly from their links with Russia. The country's prospering economy and vast potential consumer market is reflected by the GDP growing at an average annual rate of seven percent since 1999.

As a result, the influx of Russian wealth continued in 2005 when nine companies alone raised $4.6 billion through Initial Public Offerings (IPO) at the LSE. But in 2006, twenty or more Russian firms are expected to sell their shares to international investors amounting to $18-25 billion. In fact, on July 18, 2006, Rosneft, Russia's third largest oil producer listed thirteen percent of its shares at the LSE. As a result of this IPO, the company was cashing in $10.4 billion to which BP contributed $1 billion Petronas of Malaysia $1.1 billion and the CNP of China $500 million. Rosneft is the biggest IPO in the history of the LSE representing a market value of $80 billion.

The large Russian money flow also benefited the Swiss offshore facilities particularly of UBS and Credit Suisse. It can be assumed that from the above mentioned Russian outflow of $102 billion about seventy percent or $71.4 billion are being the equivalent of SFr 93.5 billion were flowing through Swiss offshore channels. This discloses partially the sources of the large money inflows of the Swiss banks during the last years. But in 2005, the money flow was even stronger as UBS and Credit Suisse received from key markets in Europe, and particularly UBS from Asia, new cash of SFr 206.4 billion of which UBS shared 71.7%. Simultaneously, total assets under management of UBS and Credit Suisse increased to SFr 4.136 billion of which UBS participates with 64.1%. As a result, in 2005 a combined net profit of SFr 15.3 billion was generated of which UBS participated with 61.7%. But keen to serve the rich Russians directly in their own country, Credit Suisse established a Swiss Private Bank in Moscow in September 2006. Therefore, the Swiss financial place is dominated by UBS and Credit Suisse, while income and growth of the other Swiss banks are limited as they operate mainly domestically. However, despite the mentioned extraordinarily large money flow, the Swiss economy benefited relatively little. Subsequently, the long lasting conflict between the financial place and workplace will continue.

Today the above financial figures of Credit Suisse and UBS have only statistical value as UBS was among the world's hardest hit banks by the financial crisis further explained in the chapter "Rescuing the Swiss Bank UBS by the Swiss Government" on page 92. But more dramatic was the worldwide drop of customer assets managed by Swiss banks from SFr. 5.235 BLN 2007 to SFr 3.822 BLN 2008 or minus 27% according to the Swiss National Bank of February 2009. As more rich customers will withdraw their assets the oversized Swiss financial place must substantially reduce its overcapacities and dismiss further staff.

The following table shows partly the development of UBS customer's assets and money in- out flow 2005-2008 published by UBS and SNB.

UBS 2005 Assets under management SFr 2.527.1 BLN
UBS 2006 Assets under management SFr 3.000.0 BLN
UBS 2007 Assets under management SFr 3.265.0 BLN at June 20
UBS 2008 Assets under management SFr 2.640.0 BLN at Sept. 30
    2008 UBS lost net SFr 625.0 BLN assets or 19.1% since 2007
UBS 2005 Money inflow   SFr 148.0 BLN,
UBS 2006 Money inflow   SFr 151.7 BLN
UBS 2008 Money outflow   SFr 226.0 BLN

Luxembourg and Liechtenstein finance

The Grand Duchy of Luxembourg with an area of 2.586 square km (kilometers) is one of the world's most industrialized countries with banking, manufacturing, and tourism as its most important economic sectors. The population of about 460.000 with a per capita income of $42.040 is using French and German in official publications and schools. In the sector of banking, this small EU (European Union) country became the world's unchallenged leader of cross-border marketing of fund products in just twenty years, leaving Switzerland far behind. Why such success? Contrary to Switzerland, Luxembourg offers a very creative and economically friendly environment. There is no red tape, and it is open for any further developments in the fund trade such as Hedge Funds and so on. Besides, thanks to its EU-status, Luxembourg-based fund products can be marketed in the EU everywhere without the approval of other EU countries. Despite the special EU-status of Luxemburg it was also classified by the OECD as a tax haven and forced to adopt the OECD Standards which it did on March 13, 2009 by waiving off the former banking secrecy.

Lichtenstein is an independent principality and a constitutional monarchy, and it is governed by a hereditary prince. With an area of 160 square km. Lichtenstein is one of the smallest independent states in the world and highly industrialized. However, much of the principality's income is derived from banking and tourism. The official language of the population of about 34.000 is German. Lichtenstein has shared many things with neighboring Switzerland since 1923, including a customs unity, currency, post service, an open border, and many agreements concerning foreign relations and bilateral matters. Having similar Swiss banking rules such as the Swiss Banking Secrecy but being more tax friendly and innovative, Lichtenstein attracted many rich customers, tens of thousands of investment and holding companies, and billions of capital. Although this small country stayed out of the European Union (EU) like Switzerland Lichtenstein's belonging to the European Economic Area allows it to participate in the EU's internal market thus competing also the Swiss financial place.

However, as the customers of Liechtenstein's banks are mostly Germans the stealing of data by a former employee of the LGT Bank in February 2008 and selling it to the German Tax Authorities was a big blow. Subsequently customers did withdraw much of their assets and Liechtenstein adopted also the OECD Standards on March 13, 2009.

Singapore finance

Time magazine of December 12, 2005, published a long essay by Jake Lloyd-Smith, how this financial place developed. The following partly quoted excerpts describe shortly its development since 1965:

> This tiny country of 648 square km with no natural resources, with only small industry, and a modest infrastructure was poorer than Mexico at that time. Today, the city is one of Asia's most modern metropolises with an estimated national economy of $100 billion in 2006, with estimated 4.430.000 industrious and educated people of which 77% are Chinese, 14% Malaysians, 8% Indians, and 1% others. The religions are Buddhism, Islamism, Christianity, and others. Over 90% of the population has their own homes, most of them well maintained, and superb clean apartments. After a decade of strong economic growth, per-capita income is actually over $21.500. This small nation with "Asian values"-to put the good of society above that of the individual—is a testimony to what hard work and discipline can do to improve lives.

In 2005, the economic growth of Singapore was 5.7%. The Chinese leaders, aware of the progress of Singapore, came to this country for three decades to listen, to learn, and to admire. Learning also and copying from Singapore, China has been rising in the last forty years from a development country like Singapore since 1965 to the world's third largest economy in 2008 with an annual growth rate of ten percent from 2003 to 2006 and a national income of $2.040 BLN in 2006. No wonder that the world of finance has discovered Singapore as a safe and a valuable offshore centre where UBS and Credit Suisse employ already a staff of 3.000. Besides, Singapore is determined to turn into a "knowledge island" similar to the USA and keen to maintain its good reputation by strict regulations to prevent any scandals. Result, Singapore has left behind the Swiss domestic financial place with its overpaid bank employees in 2007. Besides, during the same year Singapore's state fund supported the battered UBS by making a capital infusion of $13.0 BLN by means of a convertible loan. Credit Suisse too received $10 BLN but from the Middle East to improve the capital base.

USA Finance

2007-2008 the World's financial crises confirms that negative decisions made by business leaders have a tremendous impact on shareholders, employees, consumers, suppliers, communities, and the broader economy. The same was true of the unscrupulous sixteen CEOs of Enron. As greed dominated their daily life, they rejected business ethics and other virtues. Only one of the staff dared to uncover these wrongdoings for many years, but it was too late as silence was the rule with deadly consequences as illustrated in the next chapter:

2000-2001 Rise and Fall of ENRON

Enron's core activity was dealing and wheeling with electricity and gas. Trading with these commodities is normally a good business, demonstrated by the Swiss electricity company Laufenburg (ELG) which operates successfully throughout Europe. However, as profit margins are very thin, those acting for Enron created large volume with the help of derivatives and so called "Special Purpose Companies (SPC)". The latter were independent units operating as hidden tax shelters, profit and loss centers, and these units dealt with borrowed capital. In the last stage, the ballooning of uncontrolled transactions reached such a magnitude that the company imploded in November 2001. As a result the stock price plummeted from $85 at the end of 2000 to $1 in November 2001 when the seventh largest US concern in Houston went bankrupt. Its employees, shareholders, and many creditors who trusted Enron lost billions of US dollars, and over 4.000 jobs disappeared.

This handling was possible as Enron was not forced to consolidate and disclose the hidden "SPC" according to US-GAAP (United States Generally Accepted Accounting Principles) as it participated only with a minority shareholding in these financial vehicles. Consequently, the huge losses of many of the "SPC" and of Enron itself remained uncovered for a long time. But the way the bankrupt Enron could misuse loop holes in the US-GAAP to turn huge losses into profits resulted in a lack of confidence of the shareholders. They were further upset after large US companies admitted that they have changed also their losses into profits by "creative bookkeeping" triggering a sell-off at the stock markets worldwide. A further victim was the US Commercial Paper Market contracting thirty percent as these short term finance instruments issued by large US companies hardly found buyers. At the court in February 2006, Mark Koenig, former investor relations head of Enron, plead guilty. But he mentioned Enron's obsession to meet or beat Wall Street expectations.

Thus, he felt the ever-pressure to keep the stock price up even if he had to mislead analysts to do it. Under pressure was also Enron's staff to buy Enron stock pushed up by the top management and selling it with big profits prior to the collapse of the company leaving innocent employees and shareholders in a mess. It was a weak relief that Enron's leading wrongdoers received long-term prison sentences up to 24 years and that the founder has died already in 2006. Thus confirming Buddha's teaching that greed for transitory things is just stupid because it gives us pain.

The rise and fall of Enron, as well as of WORLDCOM, the former telecommunication star and second biggest US bankruptcy, and other US corporate failures alarmed the markets, the universities, the US legislation, and the security Exchange Commission (SEC), the supervising body of the New York Stock Exchange (NYSE). They set up laws and rules such as the Sarbanes-Oxley Act which encourages freedom of expression in the workplace and protects critical employees or whistleblowers uncovering wrongdoings and scandals. In particular, it ruled that all companies quoted at the American Stock Exchange must set up a hotline enabling whistleblowers to report anonymously. Moreover, some US companies have even hired ethics officers, having full power to investigate anywhere and to fire any CEO if necessary. In fact, in a working climate where employees are happy and can coexist without fear and where freedom of expression is not suppressed, team-work, creativity, and productivity in the workplace improved substantially. Well know examples of companies confirming this statement are BOEING and especially Citigroup illustrating the astonishing effect of the implementation of rules of conduct in the United States.

2005-2008 Rise and Fall of Citigroup
2005 2006 Rise of Citigroup

In February 2005 the new CEO Chuck Prince of the Citigroup—2005 the world's largest bank with a staff of 375.000, with 200 MLN customer accounts that do business in more than 100 countries—had enough from the recent scandals such as the high-profile bound trading debacle in Europe and the loss of the private banking license in Japan due to wrongdoings. So he sent out a memo to all Citigroup staff containing a five-point plan to impose company ethics published in the *Bangkok Post* on February 18, 2005 as follows:

Focus on training, improve communications, develop talent, alter performance appraisals and compensations, and strengthen control.

Attend mandatory ethics training annually, and the bank is to set up an "ethics hotline" where staff could raise issues.

Strengthen the bank's independent controls, putting extra resources into compliance and audit, and create a new structure to be called the Independent Global Compliance to be implemented throughout the company to support the business in their efforts to grow responsibility, minimize mistakes, and to ensure when mistakes occur, they are handled appropriately.

Strengthen the rules on stock ownership, insisting that near 3000 senior managers hold at least 25% of the company shares they received. Citigroup's top tier of management is already required to keep 75% of their stock

Compensation to business heads will be tied more closely to the performance of Citigroup overall rather than the unit they manage.

Senior management will also be subject to annual anonymous feedback from their staff and the appraisal process will be sharpened with a more consistent review process across the bank.

Only one year later the above guidelines encouraging employees to raise ethical issues and make wrongdoings in the workplace more difficult did bear fruit. The Global Finance Finance's editorial board selected Citigroup as the World's Best Banks based on performance over the past year and other criteria such as market leadership, customer service, competitive pricing, and innovative technologies honoring all of Citigroup's employees. The company won also a total of nine awards globally in six different categories such as Cash Management, Risk Management, Best Bank for payments and Collections and so on, making Citigroup the top in number of awards won in 2006. Financially, it achieved in 2005 a net profit of $24.6 BLN and in 2006 a net profit of still $21.6 BLN.

2007-2008 Fall of Citigroup

In spring 2008 the new CEO Vikram Pandit, of the world's 2nd largest bank —with a staff of 352.000 as of September 30, 2008, with 200 MLN customers' accounts that do business in more than hundred countries––had other news to announce than his former colleague Chucke Prince. In the Citigroup's annual repot of 2007 CEO Pandit explained that the year 2007 was marked by both great successes and significant disappointments. Many of the large businesses generated record results but were overshadowed by unprecedented losses from sudden and severe deterioration in the US sub-prime market.

In 2007 these losses combined with higher credit costs in the US consumer business drove a sharp decline in net profit dropping to $3.6 BLN or 83% .Therefore he raised in the market $30 BLN, decreased the dividend and will capture gains from the rising affluent new middle class in the emerging countries by means of credit and payment vehicles and credit cards. With the focus on excellence in productivity, efficient use of capital, operating excellence and making sure the right people are in the right place CEO Pandit cited the measures needed to achieve these targets in a difficult environment in his five-point plan for 2008 as follow:

Capital allocation—this has top priority to strengthen and reshaping risk philosophy by having the best risk management in business by eliminating low-return and non strategic assets. Furthermore positions in mortgage-backed securities and other low returning assets were sold or decreased.

Operation—Core priorities are strong expense management making Citigroup simpler, leaner, and more efficient.

Client relationship—Citigroup has been serving clients since 1812 and will making financial matters better and easier for them. The marketplace is becoming ever more complex, a situation encouraging relationship with City which the bank enjoys round the world.

Technology—Key to deepening client relationship will be the benefits of emerging technology by responding quicker, communicate more effectively and innovate faster will be able to drive superior service. In the 1970s Citigroup Chairman said: "Information about money is as important as money itself".

Talent—The difference between success and failure in financial services is the quality of the people who work with the clients. Talents have to be managed even more effectively by rewarding demonstrated performance. For this reason a talent officer was mandated to find, track and deploy the best talent. By encouraging respect, teamwork, and supportive culture that drives excellence in performance, Citigroup wants to be the financial services industry's employer of choice.

However, the best plans and best intentions fail if the world's economies and stock markets turn into a severe recession. But the worst was Citigroup's strong commitment in the US real estate and sub prime market with outstanding asset backed mortgages (ABM) of $300 BLN resulting from the securitization becoming uncontrollable. In 2008 the deterioration of the sub prime market continued resulting in the 3rd quarter to a further loss of $2.8 BLN compared to a net profit of $2.21 BLN a year before. The accumulated losses of the four quarters amounted to $20.2 BLN. Therefore the US treasury bought from Citigroup $25 BLN and later additionally $20 BLN perpetual pref. stock and warrant. But Citigroup's announcement that the workforce will be reduced to 300.000 until the end of 2008 was a surprise and shocked the markets and Citigroup's shares were traded like hot potato.

Therefore the shares plunged within one week by 60% or total 93% since the outbreak of the financial crises thus reducing the market capitalization to $20 BLN. Now the US government interfered quickly and decided to guarantee Citigroup's outstanding loans of $300 BLN. This bold and surprising US interference impressed the world's stock markets and Citigroup's stock moved within days like a rollercoaster from $3.50 to $8.29 but only dropping again to below one Dollar

Even with the backing of the US Government Citigroup's outlook is still uncertain. Nevertheless, it will continue to help the US real estate owners to solve their problems. In fact in 2007 Citigroup supported 370.000 families with mortgages of $35 BLN to keep their houses. By means of a new program other 130.000 home owners will receive mortgages of $20 BLN and experts will help them to work out individual solutions such as lower interest rates, delay for amortization etc. Furthermore for 500.000 households the company is offering financial assistance in case of need. Such steps will pay off. Besides, since CEO Prince did implement the rules 2005 nothing negatively is heard from Citigroup. Now can CEO Pandid who was surprised by the fast downturn of the world's economies and US real estate market further fully count on his staff "being extraordinary in their dedication and efforts to strengthen the company thus the power of the Citigroup brand remains unparalleled in the world as stated in the company's 2007 annual report"? Pandid has no doubts and therefore is looking forward to leading this great company.

Conclusion of Swiss and Foreign Finance
Despite Citigroup's cited problems the fife points-strategy plans of CEO Prince 2005 and CEO Pandid 2007 incl. rewarding good performance should also be an example to motivate the decision makers of the 320 Swiss domestic banks employing around 120.000 co-workers. Instead, of looking at international examples, they ignore the fact that more than twenty five percent of all Swiss bank employees do not feel well in the workplace according to the Swiss banking personnel union (SBPV) when meeting with journalists on January 28, 2006. They complain the pressure to perform better and especially the incompetence of managers who are against freedom of expression as they fear their professional weakness and deficiencies could be uncovered. But the worst Swiss banking crises 2007-2008 changed dramatically the life of managers and employees. Therefore the following statement of Micheal Catalanello, in his essay "Is your workplace psychologically healthy"? is still valid published in the *Pattaya Mail* of Thailand dated March 17, 2006, and quoted as follow:

Employees who are consulted by management and involved in decision making process usually feel more empowered in their work. Another way of encouraging further psychological health in the workplace is to provide regular opportunities for employees to upgrade their job related knowledge and skills by offering work place in-services, tuition reimbursement, leadership- and career development. Management recognition of employees for outstanding contributions for the company can also promote psychologically health in the workplace.

In fact it is terrible to work for envious and selfish managers and third parties. It is worse if the staff must silently accept wrongdoings of all kinds—including invasion of privacy in the workplace. Still worse is the fact that any such uncovering is treason of internal affairs and should not be protected according to the president of the Swiss Banking Association (SBV) and other Swiss bankers as reported in the *Swiss Moneycab* of September 7, 2005.

However, the above statement differs from a big advertisement of five Swiss private banks in the French part of Switzerland published in the NZZ of 2001 stating that "Privacy is for mankind as important as oxygen for the nature". And in January 2006 professor Vischer of the World Health Organization (WHO), Geneva, mentioned: "Privacy is a high personality asset". Therefore any invasion of privacy coupled with forceful suppression and intimidation should be uncovered and investigated.

London is the worlds' second largest financial place with a unique tax system attracting wealthy people and billions of Dollars of capital. With worldwide six top universities with brand names like Oxford, Cambridge, London School of Economics etc., they attract the brightest students and create first-class graduates. Thus, they also achieve outstanding result in the London financial place with international banks like Great Britain's number one, HSBC, disclosing in 2005 a net profit of $21.0 billion and in the first half of 2006—a net profit of $12.5 billion. But due to the world's banking crisis 2007-2008 HSBC too lost single digit billions 2008. Smaller and younger Luxembourg developed much faster than the older and bigger Swiss financial place. The latter has already lost ground and competences in 2005 to its competitors in the fund business and formerly in the F/X trade and in the European bond market. And finally, creative Lichtenstein offers additional advantages thanks to its participation of the European Union's international market.

The extraordinarily fast development of the Asian countries since the early 60s to worldwide top key players was achieved without large money injections: It was the result of an industrious population with strong values and the ethos to learn from others and to work hard. Thanks to surging exports, Asia's foreign exchanges reached $1.600 billion or nearly forty percent of the world's total reserves of which China has $1000 billion, Singapore $115 billion and South Korea $205.8 billion.

Result: In the large and sophisticated world of finance, thousands of banks nationally and internationally protect and motivate the staff to uncover wrongdoings in the workplace for the sake of the banks' customers, shareholders and reputation. Therefore "whistleblowers should also be protected in Switzerland" warns MP R. Gysin in the Swiss parliament published by the *NZZ* of September 22, 2005. He further requested that the Swiss Government should create and set up an appropriate law. His claim was supported by an article in the *NZZ* of October 9, 2006, stating that "in Switzerland too, there is a big necessity to uncover illegal and unethical practices of employers". This statement is documented by the Transparency International which registered 25 cases of wrongdoings alone in the first six months of 2006. However, it did not interfere as the concerned co-workers have angst and fear to get harassed und fired by their employers. But in Switzerland where freedom of expression is suppressed in the workplace and international rules of conduct such as the SEC-Sarbanes-Oxley Act are disregarded and rejected the past and recent scandals will not be stopped. Finally in 2009 the Swiss Justice Department will work out appropriate laws to protect whistleblowers but they will be much less strict than in the USA. In view of the above the Swiss Banking Association's president plans that small Switzerland should become a world leader also in research and teaching will be a dream forever. This is also underlined by the investigations of the World Economic Forum respectively WEF giving Switzerland not the best rankings on their world's banking ranking list. Besides, Switzerland's adoption of the OECD Standards on March 13, 2009, replacing the lucrative banking secrecy will making the formerly disadvantaged banks more competitive.

VI.
SWISS and Foreign Ethics and Morals

According to Buddha, decay of good manners lead to delusion triggering greed and hate, and thus to economic ruin.
In the year 2004, the daily newspaper, *Bangkok Post*, wanted to know from its readers which of the characteristics such as responsibility, consciousness, punctuality, integrity, ethics, morals, self discipline, loyalty, modesty, helpfulness and so on are the most important virtues. Eighty percent of the readers decided upon ethics and morals. Consequently when the formerly popular Prime Minister, Thaksin Shinavatra, founder of the Thai Rak Thai (Thai love Thai) party, was finally accused for alleged corruption, conflict of interest, abuse of power, and intimidating the press he lost the confidence of many Thais. Subsequently he stepped down from office after a meeting with the King in April 2006. Being still a burden for the country he was overthrown in a bloodless coup on September 20, 2006, and replaced on October 1, 2006 by a former Thai general as interim prime minister. It was the first coup after 15 years but necessary according to the Thai Army Commander in Chief to "heal the mounting rifts in Thai society and to end government corruption".

In February 2008 a democratic government was elected and the Thai Rak Thai party achieved an excellent result but lost the majority anyway despite it changed the name to "Peoples Power Party". 2007 Thaksin exiled to London where he owns real estates. In addition he bought the well known football club Manchester City and returned in March 2008 to Thailand to defend his case at the court which condemned his wife on July 31, 2008, to prison charges in connection with a real estate scandal. By means of a special permission he visited the Olympic Games in Peking but instead to return to Thailand he went back with his wife to England again. There he applied for a visa but was refused. On November 15, 2008, he divorced after 32 years of marriage. "May be for convenient reason" remarked Bloomberg's.

speaker on the TV. Thaksin's behavior was neither in line with Buddha's teaching—"driving out each kind of ego"—nor with Confucius' teaching—"putting the society above family relationships". It was the big ethical and moral power of the Thai king and the Thais' strong belief in Buddha's teachings that let to this bloodless coup. Buddha's teaching is further explained in the German essay "Human Being Buddha" by Ludwig Hasler published in the Swiss "*Weltwoche*" of August 6, 2005, of which the excerpts are quoted as follow:

In Buddhism the vicious circle begins with delusion, thus puts greed and hate into operation, and these stabilize the delusion. The intellectual arrogance of the Brahmans displeases Buddha. They speculate upon the nature of reality, the appointment of the soul, as if they can see everywhere behind it. Buddha looks on the surface of human everyday existence: how humans entangle themselves in their demand for inconsistent things, in disappointment and in fear and anger. He sees the release from this suffering as the only desirable and worthwhile goal. Thus, Buddha wants to eliminate suffering, not console us, and he teaches that greed is stupid because it gives us pain.

The soul is not a firm core for Buddha; it has no substance and moves from one body to the next. He sees it rather as a fluid form of energy quantum, mental as well as sentimental. As long as these energies are not used up, they search for new activation. This is the idea behind reincarnation and quantum physics. The cycle of life (Samsara), equated by Buddha with the suffering from the desires and urges should be broken through the Nirvana which is the emptiness, in which reincarnation is finally stopped. Nirvana does not mean that there is nothing in contrast to existence, rather, that all and nothing are in contrast to existence. Without responding, there is no movement. Where there is no movement, there is peace. Where there is peace, there is no desire. Where there is no desire, there is no coming and going; there is no dying and no birth. No here, no there and nothing in between. That is suffering's end. Buddha does not teach one to turn away from the world. He only advises one not to rely on pieces of wealth, possession, and reputation.

The above teaching illustrates with relentless openness how Buddhism condemns the egocentric striving for transitory things and describes three aspects of the unhappy egoists: greed, hate, and delusion. This is because nature is always moving and never finds peace as it wants. This applies even with criminal energy more and more, unless an accident, illness or event forcibly brings to an end this striving for money and property. Such materialism spoils the character and allows good customs and ethical and moral doubts to disappear. That is the ideal beginning for envy, greed, and craving for recognition to grow from.

In fact, the Roman republic from 509 to 27 BC was dead after internal unrest. Recovering as a Roman monarchy led by emperors from 27 BC to 476 AD, the Roman Empire fell finally due to internal unrest. Additionally, economic, ethic, and moral decline coupled with the German invasion destroyed the formerly strong Roman armies. And today, some saturated Western European countries, including Switzerland with growth rates of only one or two percent as many reforms are still pending can withstand and match only the industrious and innovative nations from Asia and Eastern Europe by means of trade barriers and economic sanctions.

So for example in the Czech Republic car workers earn around $6.2 a hour. In China labor costs at car plants are around $1.37 a hour which is around fifty times lower than in Western Germany. And where do co-workers enjoy the longest annual holidays? In France: 31 days, Germany: 29 days, Swiss finance industry: 25.5 days, Eastern Europe's Estonia and Lithuania: 19 days, Latvia: 15 days, and the USA: 13 days. Stiffer competition, creation of innovative products, new services and keen for a better living drive Americans to work harder while the poorer Asians make even bigger sacrifices for a better living. No wonder that in 2015 Asia's economies will account 45% of the world's GDP, significantly more than the USA and Europe combined shown by the following GDP figures: China: 20%, India: 8%, Japan: 6%, other Asia: 11% versus Western Europe: 17%, USA: 20%, and the rest of the world: 18%, forecasted by the Australian Government published in *The Economist* of 18 March 2006.

Teaching of Buddhism and Teaching of Christianity

Buddhism's teaching is not a religion like Christianity and Islam. Rather it is a plan to live the life in such a way to win the highest reward. For Buddhists, the emptiness of nirvana will finally be the end of all suffering and bring happiness. Christianity, however, teaches that only in heaven with God and Jesus Christ mankind can find real happiness. But both Buddhism and Christianity teach us "that no soul can ever reach this final spiritual target if good virtues have been disregarded as a human being on earth". Both Buddhist and Christian teachings condemn despicable ethical and moral behavior, as well as greed. They consider what use it is to the human being if he/she wins the whole world and his/her soul suffers harm.

For the Christian teaching envy is labeled as one of the worst of the seven deadly sins. It was the sin of envy which brought death into the world. The holy Augustine, Italian bishop and church teacher of the fourth century, saw the devilish sin in envy as absolute. No other movement of the soul generates such immense bad feelings—even hate, slander, joy in the misfortune of others, and displeasure in his/her well-being. The German theologian and philosopher, Antje Schrupp, considered envy one of the broadest, and at the same time, most commonly denied feelings.

And Joseph Deiss, former president and member of the Swiss Federal Government who resigned in April 2006, made critical remarks about the widespread envy in Switzerland where Christianity is the state religion. So he said among other things in his speech to the Swiss people of August 1, 2004, the Swiss National Day: "I sometimes have the impression that at some places the increasing insular infightings and intended provocations mean that the Confederation is lived out as an Envy-Confederation where everyone only thinks of himself leading to an unhealthy egoism where community spirit has been lost".

The power of Asian values

The partly quoted excerpts of a lengthy German report published in the Swiss *Weltwoche* of July 2006 are based on the book "Japan versus China in the industrial Race" by Wei-Bin Zhang 1998. They answer the question: What made the peoples of China since 1965, Vietnam since 1972, South Korea since 1953 and Japan since 1945 so strong to emerge from poverty up to economic power houses with a combined national economy of $7.870 billion in 2006 despite the countries were suffering from natural disasters, hunger, war and political unrest?

It was mainly the teaching of Confucius who was born in the province Shandong 650 years BC. His values were learning common sense and having respect for elderly people. God was unknown to him as his obligation was to behave ethically correctly. Besides, that the individual should not be in the focus but instead focus on the society which he put above family relationships. The individual has to subordinate his personal requirement to those of the family where sons, even grown-up, were strongly committed to their fathers, and the wife to her husband. Confucius denied a system of social classes and materialistic wealth. And pretenders disgusted him because the real sense of the human being is to have a good character. The Confucianism society model in China, Vietnam and Korea is the family and in Japan the household. The family members are kept together by having the same blood. In Japan the society model is the household to which the couple is committed. This is for the Japanese the right place which can also be a group of people, the school, and the company to which he is generally a loyal life time worker.

In China the role of Confucius teaching is different. For the Chinese parents the most important thing is to provide their children the best education regardless the costs. Sons and daughters having diplomas from universities are the parent's biggest pride. Chinese do not consider the working life as a continued career as it will change anyway. Therefore they are very flexible and react much faster to changed conditions. Chinese do not contradict their parents, but their loyalty in their family hierarchy is not so strong like in the Confucianism dominated Korea and Japan.

However, contrary to the two latter nations, the Chinese loyalty goes to family members living far away worldwide like a clan who have emigrated since the 19th century first to Vietnam and North America. The Chinese clans have built up a global net supporting each other. Since the 1980s when China gave up its isolation, the overseas Chinese were quickly ready to operate as informal investment and export channels. The large money flow from Hong Kong family clans was crucial for the fast growth of the Chinese economy. The fact that small Chinese entrepreneurs do not receive bank credits it is normally the extended Chinese family providing financial support even if the project is risky or may fail. But if a project is flourishing, the family clan as a whole is benefiting from the success. Result: the combination of millions of hard working entrepreneurs coupled with the above mentioned values supported by their family clans made China what it is today. The same is true for the other three Asian countries having the same ethics and morals. These four nations with future strong growths rates will be not far away in 2015 to match the US national economy of presently $13.153 billion.

South Korean Working Ethics

The *Magazine Fortune* of September 2, 2005, published a report of Peter Lewis of Samsung's history and management culture. It is a further typical example of power of Asian values in the practice and deserves to be mentioned. In fact, what are the secrets of the turnaround of the electronic company, Samsung? The quoted excerpts give the answer:

In 1969 Samsung started in a simple Quonset hut. There it made the first cheap black and white TV and other knockoff products to be sold in convenience stores. But after many years of success, supply far outstripped demand in 1996, and the fifteen percent rise of the Korean won in 1997 nearly destroyed Samsung. In this difficult time, the sixty-one year old engineer and CEO, Jong-Yong Yun, said in his monthly speech to the company: "either we are becoming a world leader or a major failure". Simultaneously, he was preaching to the work force the following guide lines:

- The bigger barrier to management innovation is— the ego—a self that never changes.

- You do not predict the future and then wait—You create the future.
- We cannot live without change—The race for survival in this world in not to the strongest, but to the most adaptive.
- Quality is the conscience of a company—It is the reason for the company's existence.
- The core of an electronics company is technology— You cannot survive without the ability to develop products independently.

Now Samsung Electronics is one of the most innovative, respected, and profitable players in the consumer-electronics and semiconductors. In 2005, its OfficeServ 7200 product was honored with the "Product of the Year" awarded by the Inter@action Solution Magazine, Richardson, Texas. From 2002 to 2006 Samsung won 19 Industrial Design Excellence Awards (IDEAs) compared to 15 of Apple, 12 of Hewlet-Packard and 10 of IBM. In 2004, the company earned $11.8 BLN and sales reached $121.7 BLN surpassing Sony despite this company was in 1969 already a global brand when Samsung was a startup firm in a Quonset hut. In line with Samsung's success, South Korea's national economy has reached $785 BLN in 2006 after the GDP soared by 5.2% in the fourth quarter of 2005. After being successful until 2007 Samsung as an export company feels also the global downturn of the economy 2008. Nevertheless, Samsung will master the world's economic crises like in 1997 with new and highly innovative products.

The Power of Western Values
As mentioned above one of Asia's values are the close family relationships and the worldwide Chinese family clans supporting industrious but poor family entrepreneurs. But who supports Western entrepreneurs having little or no resources? The following quoted excerpts of the lengthy reports of "the rise of social entrepreneurs" and "Virtue's intermediaries", published in The Economist of February 25, 2006, describe briefly the virtue's Western financial backers.

> In the Western world and elsewhere bright social entrepreneurs seldom or exceptionally receive family support. In fact in the book "The power of Ideas" David Bornstein confirmed this lack of support although "entrepreneurs are transformative forces with new ideas to address major problems and who are relentless in the pursuit of their vision".

Furthermore, according to management guru Peter Drucker "entrepreneurs are also risk takers and people with ideas who raise the performance capacity of society". Connecting these Western entrepreneurs with rich donators such as Western philanthropists and Western non-profit organizations with good virtues has become a multibillion US Dollar business. Today, the number of financial backers with non profit and charity character has increased to more than 1.4 million worldwide. A well-know example is the International Red Cross headquartered in the Swiss city of Geneva distributing its collected money to people suffering from war and disasters. Another intermediary located in Geneva is "Geneva Global" covering opportunities in outside America. GG's 140 employees work of over 500 voluntary associates in over 100 countries. It mostly concentrates on small projects, which it thinks have a greater impact by finding a small local group that is doing something well and is ready to scale up its opportunities in the business and in the social sectors.

People working for non-profits—to make incomes that are at least equal to outgoings—do not work to make just money but to make a difference. An example is the non-profit *Teach for America* founded 1989. This organization gets graduates from top universities to spend the first two years of their career teaching children from low income families. In 2005 it has received 97.000 applications, but only 14.000 had been accepted. The social sectors do not have rational capital markets to channel resources to those who deliver the best results. Consequently financial costs of donated capital in the USA can soar up to twenty-two percent to forty-three percent while in Britain the average financial costs are around twenty-five percent. The latter depend on the brand name as the world of giving is favoring family organizations such as the Red Cross, Ford and Gate foundations and Rockefeller Family Advisors.

Driven by growing demand due to growing enthusiasm of the rich for philanthropy, together with their determination to see their money used to better effect, has prompted talk of a new "golden age of philanthropy". No wonder that banks such as Goldman Sachs, HBSC, Coutts and UBS are now also scaling up philanthropy advisory services.

UBS as the biggest and formerly the best Swiss bank with business ethics, that counts many of the world's richest people among its clients, is conducting an interesting experiment. So it was forming an alliance with Ashoka, founded 1980, which is a global organization that identifies and invests in leading social entrepreneurs in Brazil, Mexico and Argentina. Different is the purpose of the newly formed Swiss Elea Foundation for "Ethics in Globalization" created by the Ex-UBS-CEO Peter Wuffli and his wife Susanne.

Its focus is the "promotion of knowledge of economically interconnections in Switzerland and to fight directly against poverty abroad resulting from globalization". Goldman Sachs created the "New Philanthropy Capital (NPC)" to get the holy grail of new givers for charitable donations and providing "buy" recommendations through sector reports. Such consulting services are crucial for all kind of donators who want that their money is invested wisely. Therefore skills, knowledge, and experience are needed to find the right balance between risks and opportunities for the sake of all parties. This is different to the "Chinese way of financing" where family members accept failures of their family entrepreneurs.

Without ethical and moral parameters, everything is permitted
Because these guidelines are missing or ignored in the Credit Suisse Group, the second largest Swiss bank has more scandals than any other Swiss bank. On the other hand, one heard until 2007 rarely anything negative from the UBS, the formerly most prominent Swiss bank. What is the reason for this? In the UBS co-workers had to sign a compliance sheet to behave ethically and morally correctly. Other Swiss banks have house rules or approaches in place in order to clarify boundaries and eliminate inconsistencies. This could be the reason that the legislator did not yet legally embody ethical and moral principles. However, in cases where nothing is regulated in a company, no restraining threshold hinders bad behavior of co-workers, directors of the board, and CEOs. In the cases of UBS and Credit Suisse corporate government rules did exist but were just ignored as greed prevailed with catastrophically consequences. The following chapters illustrate the development from inconsistencies to scandals.

1977 The Chiasso-Scandal of Credit Suisse

In March 1977, the Chiasso scandal of the Credit Suisse Bank took the public by surprise. The credit Suisse branch in Chiasso announced first a loss of SFr. 400 MLN. At that time, Chiasso was the most successful branch, and the branch manager was a celebrated banker. But the losses continued to rise until the sum of SFr. 1.3 BLN was finally reached. Subsequently, at the Swiss Stock Exchange the bank's shares were traded like hot potatoes.

What had happened? The Italians had no confidence in their own currency and brought bags of lira notes into Switzerland and also to the Chiasso branch where the Swiss manager did not disclose the received cash in the balance sheet. Nevertheless, the customers were given a document guaranteeing interest and a return of money in Swiss Francs. Thereafter billions of Lira cash were transferred to a newly created Swiss holding and investment company in Liechtenstein, which invested it in hotels, vineyards, and real estates in Italy. The case blew up when the extension of the deficit in warranty obligations and invested capital was revealed. Then in Chiasso three positions for directors became free, and this branch of Credit Suisse became a successful real estate company. It was successful because, according to rumors, the increases in value of the real estates covered the Chiasso losses to a large extent. The result was delusion which produced greed leading to these crimes and an ensuing cover-up.

1997-2002 An unfortunate CEO and President
of the Credit Suisse Group

January 1997
Lukas Mühlemann became CEO and President
of the Credit Suisse Group

December 9, 1997
Effective date of the takeover of the Winterthur Insurance Company by the Credit Suisse Holding. Procedure of the transaction: one reg. share of Winterthur was changed into 7.3 reg. shares of CS Holding. Mühlemann was initially against this deal, his thinking was: why buy the cow when one can have the milk without. Nevertheless, he bought the overpriced Winterthur anyway and helped the Swiss investor Ebner to make a super profit with his stake of thirty percent of Winterthur because he pushed the shares up to eighty percent in recent years.

September 1998
Crisis in Asia and Russia makes losses of SFr. 1.9 billion.

May 1999
Credit Suisse scandal in Japan. Numerous reproaches of the national supervising board of the FSA due to insufficient control structures, lack of information from the management and so on.

May 2000
Rainer Gut resigned as president of the board and Mühlemann takes over the presidency.

July 2001
The restructuring of the group of early 1997 was changed again.

October 2, 2001
Grounding of all Swissair planes worldwide and mutual debt assignments followed on the part of the banks UBS, Credit Suisse and Swissair. This was due to Swissair board members and representatives of Swissair's house bank and Mühlemann, being made jointly responsible for disastrously wrong decisions during the last years.

January 2002
Credit Suisse must pay a fine of $100 million to the NY Stock Exchange Commission (SEC) due to dodgy practices at the Credit Suisse First Boston, New York. They had been offering customers, so called, "attractive IPOs" which were, in fact, junk papers.

June 2002
Winterthur Insurance needs a capital infusion of SFr. 1.7 billion.

September 2002
Leaves Credit Suisse at the end of the year and CEO Kielholz of Swiss Re, becomes president of the board.

Műhlemann underestimated the task of being a CEO in a complex worldwide banking group. The spontaneous shift of opinion with the Winterthur takeover alone cost Credit Suisse billions. Very hasty restructurings and acquisitions also made the CS Group a "large-scale building site" thus absorbing further billions. He urgently needed a partner in the presidency, but instead he took it over himself. After the turbulences of the recent years, the Credit Suisse Group eagerly polished its image. Added to this, a new logo was created although the blue and red Credit Suisse logo was introduced only eight years previously. Subsequently for the 150 years jubilee of 2006 the Credit Suisse integrated all former independent bank units into one bank concern with one new logo focusing on Investment Banking, Private Banking, and Asset Management. The new logo with stylized sails should mirror the spirit which is the Credit Suisse Concern of today and what it wants to be in future: The break with the past is obviously intended because the Műhlemann era was so disastrous and unique that it will be remembered for a long time. As a result of the new business strategy, the Winterthur insurance company was upgraded and sold to the French Insurance company AXXA, the world's second largest insurance company, at a price of SFr. 12.5 billion in June 2006 but much less than the acquisition costs. This was the end of the "All Finance Concept" which was a wrong strategy and an illusion to make big money.

1755-1990 Rise and Fall of the Swiss Private Bank Leu
The following interesting quoted excerpts of a Credit Suisse Holding report and excerpts from the holocaust investigations describe the history and preparations to takeover a bank possessing the potential to become a top Swiss bank but failed.

1755-1918 Swiss Bank's successful development
The bank was founded by its first president and mayor of Zurich Johann Jakob Leu. As a state bank under the name of "Leu et Compagnie" it issued bonds to rich Zurich citizens for their entrusted money which in turn was lent to the international markets. 1798 France occupied parts of Switzerland and the bank went private thus preventing to be taken over by the new Helvetic Government. 1854 the bank was changed to Aktiengesellschaft Leu & Co. 1855 it took part in the extraordinary industrial upswing by financing industrial projects, electricity plants, railways and hotels.

1939-1945 Swiss Bank's Development prior and after World War II
Switzerland's politically and economically stability, neutrality, discretion and uncomplicated handling of financial transactions attracted foreign capital. The latter gained increasingly importance after 1914 which led to the legalization of the Swiss banking secrecy 1934. The big money flow enabled Swiss banks to make big investments in countries paying higher interest including Germany. With the NS regime on power 1936 the SBG, SBC & CS's assets in Germany were substantial. In the case of the Swiss Bank they reached 27% of total assets. Worried of the politically unstable Germany the Swiss banks silently agreed 1931 that the German debtors were granted six months delays for short term loans generating much higher interest income. These temporary agreements were regularly renewed in the following 14 years enabling the NS regime to waive off the repayments due on the expiration dates. The NS regime cultivated a close friendly- and even fellow-like business relationship with the neutral Swiss financial place. But later the total writing off of the German credits hit the Swiss Bank particularly hard. Having no other choice like SBG, SBC & CS the Swiss Bank was now fully depending on the development in Germany and made risky financial transactions in the hope this country will succeed. But the stop of the German money flow let to the end of the bank which survived only thanks to the strong support of the Swiss Bank Corporation merging later with SBG to UBS. Paying a very high price for the wrong and ill fated strategy the heavily battered bank operated afterwards only in Zurich and its surroundings by waiving off new adventures abroad.

1980s Swiss Bank's Raiders targeted the bank to take it over
Politically and economically weakened the Swiss bank could not participate anymore in the unprecedented boom in the years after World War II 1939-1945 like the three big Swiss banks UBS, SBC and Credit Suisse. Even in Zurich the Swiss bank could hardly compete with other banks and thus was not much of interest for qualified top mangers and staff. Instead the Swiss bank positions were occupied by less qualified managers cashing high salaries, looking more for themselves and unable to make the bank competitive and profitable being called in the market "neither fish nor bird". Due to divergences and changes in the top management the Swiss Bank was encircled by takeover raiders including the well known financier Martin Ebner with his BZ Bank. The winner was CEO R. Gut of the Credit Suisse Holding for strategically reasons. Consequently he was highly interested to buy this bank and offered the top management to keep their positions and the Swiss Bank's independence within the Credit Suisse Group.

1990 Swiss Bank's Takeover announced at the General Meeting
By officially informing the shareholders on March 29, 1990, of the new majority shareholder the weak top management was very happy that now the CS Holding is taking care of the "Leu patient". This was for reasons as false promises have been made. In fact a few months later fraudulent activity in a branch costing SFr. 61 MLN–which was for many years uncovered–"coincidentally" came to surface. At the end of 1990, the Swiss bank's official financial statements disclosed that the bank lost over SFr 100 MLN which was covered by realizing core participations of SFr 204 MLN in the balance sheet. Besides, the financial statements further disclosed that during the last seven years the management put an estimated SFr. 14.4 million into their own pockets. The IT plants had to be replaced, and the bank's assets under management did not meet the great expectations. Consequently, if the markets had known these facts prior to the takeover Swiss bank's stock would have plunged like stones. Therefore CS-Holding paid an exorbitant price for the Swiss Bank's stock despite the takeover of the Swiss bank was strategically clever. Worse afterwards it was a twelve year long expensive exercise coupled with many management changes to achieve finally the turnaround in 2003 with new decision makers.

1989-2003 Swiss Bank's Violation of Rules of Conduct & Ethics
This chapter demonstrates the manner in which Swiss managers took advantage of having no laws or guidelines in place to investigate violation of ethics and morals. Worse was that an instance or institution also to probe such wrongdoing was planned by the government and discussed in the Swiss parliament for six year. Additionally, no internal rules of conduct existed in this bank. Instead forced silence and freedom of expression were suppressed. In fact, friends and former employees were not allowed to talk with the author even years after his departure of the bank despite the bank benefited a lot from his extra work and knowledge without compensation. Due to bad rumors in the market, the anxious management was cultivating corporatism by promoting friends and selected employees providing information.

Collecting all kind of information for a weak management and others was and is often for some employees more rewarding than working. But only employees with bad virtues, professional deficiencies and the inability to work independently would harass co-workers and operate like spies. In such a working environment every qualified co-worker is a potential enemy who could hinder the wrongdoers' future career.

To cover their weakness they copy another's work and libel co-worker. And worse, they start violation and invasion of privacy. By squeezing co-workers respectively "potential enemies" out of the company, such unqualified bank servant's achieve a short term sweet victory. But the company suffers a long term bitter defeat as skilled personnel is the most valuable human capital. True is also that such people are eager to show off themselves in the profession, in the media and elsewhere. Acting like confidence trickster they pretend to be someone they would like to be. Exceeding by far their personal skills and capacity they develop often criminal energies in the hope to succeed but to the disadvantage of others. Such persons are also unable to build up "Emotional Quotient" (EQ) as mentioned earlier and explained and published in the *Pattaya Mail* of Thailand, dated June 9, 2006, based on the Daniel Coleman's Emotional Quotient (EQ), in neuroscience and psychology. The excerpts from it are quoted and detailed as follow:

> Emotional Quotient (EQ) is our emotional intelligence which determines our potential for learning the practical skills. They are based on its five elements: self-awareness, self-discipline, self-motivation, empathy and flexibility. Therefore people having little or no potential for learning the practical skills have a low EQ. Consequently they are not creative, not entrepreneurial and reform hostile thus unqualified for leading and teaching positions. In practice such people prefer to cultivate the splendid standstill in companies and elsewhere. As a result they adversely affect growth, competitiveness and profitability of companies ending up as typical takeover candidates illustrated in the following example.

Fraud?

1989 the author was looking for a new challenge and met two bankers working in the same bank having a bad reputation. One was CIO and the other "chef analyst" of the investment research. Its products were substandard and of poor value for customers and investment advisors. The author wanted to help this man by building up with him a top research. But cleaning up the chaos and the creation of new products was very time consuming and could not be done within the working hours. Therefore he was also during weekends and late evenings in the bank. In fact, the "Research Division" was rather a dusty old museum store. On the floor were piles of white and brown paper clippings up to 20 years of which the brown ones were on the bottom and the dozens unclassified and wrongly labeled old packed files full of old information.

Nevertheless, the author did not receive any help from the "chef analyst" who had finally time and money to build his new house and other private work. Consequently big was the shock to learn that the author's employment as vice president had only short time character. The reason was that the CIO and the "chef analyst" hired secretly a new graduate analyst who was foreseen to replace the author when opportune. Despite these facts, the author continued to realize his plan cleaning up the mess to improve the poor research products to a satisfactory level with a time horizon of about 2½ years. But in the second phase these products should be replaced by valuable research products requiring analytical skills and professional knowledge.

Therefore customers and investment advisors estimated the author's work but he became an unwanted competitor and thus he was copied and isolated. No wonder that one day the author found in another office coincidently an opened personally addressed letter from the director of a successful European private bank summarized as follow:

> Date: March 30, 1990: "I remember you at meeting in Berne. I receive the investment reports from your bank and take the opportunity to congratulate you for the excellent work, for the clear presentation and accurate forecast. I think with such a good instrument the prospective investor has a basic tool at his disposition for investments decisions. I will mail you our annual report".

The fact that envy prevailed in this bank, the author did not reveal this letter. But in 1992, the European bank started to build up a research division of its own, waiving off the Swiss Bank's research products remaining substandard as the "chef analyst" was unable to create quality products. Nevertheless, at the end of 1990 he was promoted to manager coupled with high salaries and allowances upsetting some investment consultants at the bank's promotion party. At the beginning of October 1991 the "chef analyst" took over the author's construction work and said to the author: "You are not needed anymore" and was harassed out of the bank 1991/1992. Pretending in the bank to handle the author's job as well the "chef analyst" was further promoted to managing director by cashing top salaries in the following years until 2003 while the investment research remained unchanged.

Lacking PC- and language skills and little professional knowledge the "chef analyst" was very demanding. To cover his deficiencies he started to spy co-workers within and outside the bank including invasion of privacy of the author's wife. However, the anxious top management and the CIO estimated such secret information much more than work performance. Subsequently the "chef analyst" was allowed to copy the author's work and ordered to "qualify" him.

Eager to collect for the CIO and top management private and business information he put the author soon after his working start in May 1989 under constant pressure for a three months period to participate with his ex-wife at a dinner party at his home with his wife. After the "chef analyst" ordered: "Now you must come!" He finally gave in and discovered that he and his wife—without the author's knowledge— made a daily analysis of his professional and private life and had access to all confidential information.

Before the court in summer 1990, the author realized that his Polish ex-wife had been manipulated by others in the Swiss Bank. At the beginning of October 1991 after two and one-half years the "CIO" ordered the author in his office where he informed him that the "chef analyst" must appear at the court as a witness. The author added that in case "the chef analyst" would not appear, the police will take him into custody, "Never", said the "CIO" and was beating his fist with full force on the table. One week later, the divorce fight was over after 1½ years. The author's Polish ex-wife received far less than the author had offered her in the case of a peaceful settlement.

This court decision did not please the "CIO". Briefly, on October 18, 1991, during a three-day break of a two-week seminar of the Swiss civil service, the author was ordered again to appear in the office of the "CIO". Present at this time was also one of the personnel manager, "S", the "CIO" was sitting on the author's right side and "S" on the opposite side of the table. "S" handed a pen and a renouncement letter over to the author which he refused to read. "S" asked the author several times to sign it. As he stood up, "the CIO" shouted, "Where are you going?" The author said to make a copy. At this moment, the "CIO" grabbed his right arm with both hands and pressed him on the chair. The "CIO" shouted again, "Sign or you will be fired immediately", he refused again. After two hours of painful discussions, he was released. But in the afternoon the "CIO" came into the author's office and threatened him should anyone learn anything of this meeting. This incidence was quickly forgotten as the prevention of the Swiss banking crisis had the highest priority as illustrated in the next chapter.

1991-2005 Preventing a dramatic banking crisis

Prior to reporting of the menacing Swiss banking crisis what did happen first in the USA? In the second half of the 1980s, thousand US savings and loan banks were in trouble or went bankrupt. From 1989 to 1992, each year more than two hundred of 2.400 savings and loan banks were closed. Besides, in 1990 more than 500 commercial banks merged. What were the costs? Alone for each insured saving deposit of $100.000 the government spent $160 billion and further spent $340 billion in the next forty years for the interest of the government bonds issued to indemnify creditors. What was the reason for this disaster? It occurred because of a credit crunch due to risky and overextended financing of overvalued real estate and junk bonds coupled with soaring interest rates in an inflationary and recessive environment.

In the 1990s the Japanese companies did not learn from the US disaster. Instead they operated much worse. A typical example was "Zaitech" meaning buying stock and real estate's with borrowed cheap capital and pushing up its prices to sky heights. As a result they disclosed appropriate high non-operating paper profits.

However, not for long time as many non-competitive firms especially in the manufacturing industries were strongly subsidized by badly organized banks. These "zombie" companies damaged the profitability of healthy rivals generating really cash. Worse the "zombies" made entire industries sick as the lax Japanese banking regulations enabled the banks to throw good money at favorable conditions further to sick firms instead to cut them off. In the following ten years banks, insurance and industry companies collapsed in line with the Nikkei index of 38.915 of December 29, 1989 to a 19 year low of 8.400 in October 2002 paralyzing the economy until its recovery in 2005 but only to drop further to below 7000 points in 2009.

In 1991 Switzerland was no exception. Scarce and expensive capital invested in low-interest bearing, politically sensitive mortgages and in overvalued real estate battered the domestic banks terribly. Nevertheless, in spring 1991 the regional Swiss Saving and Loan Bank Thune (SLT) and its top managers including those of the Swiss Bank celebrated in Thune the 125 years jubilee of the SLT. Then on the very date of October 3, 1991, the Swiss regional bank made worldwide headlines in the TV and newspapers when hundreds of frustrated customers were queuing in front of the closed doors of the bank. This was the catalyst to set up an evaluation system for banks similar to the analyzing scheme for industries published in the author's book 1976.

But what surprise to discover that more than fifty regional and local banks were in the same bad shape like SLT. And this was only the tip of an iceberg. However, not any bank, Swiss National Bank, Banking Commission and not any other authority in Switzerland had knowledge of this dramatic situation. The reason was that the regional and local banks have always fulfilled their legal liquidity and equity requirements.

The author presented his homework to the top manager of the Swiss Bank who said immediately that this know how should be kept secretly, and contacted thereafter third parties to avoid a second and worse panic in the market. This was for good reason as the Swiss Bank had outstanding bank debtors of over SFr. 5 BLN and cultivated close relationships with many of these shaky regional and local banks. The same was true for the Credit Suisse, UBS and other Swiss and foreign banks. Subsequently, an UBS manager called the author "a traitor if his know how would be published as "we want an orderly withdrawal". And another UBS manager was upset at the author's investment report of May 15, 1992, recommending selling the Swiss Volksbank shares at SFr. 910 which dropped 30% after publication. But the disclosing of a huge loss for the 1st HY in July 1992, the battered bank survived only due to a spontaneous stock swap offer by the CS Holding CEO R. Gut to change the SVB shares into those of Credit Suisse. However, with Swiss Bank and Swiss Volksbank, Credit Suisse Holding was burdened with two big cost and bad loan problems. In the following years, the decision makers of the stronger banks, the Swiss National Bank and the Swiss Banking Commission acted quickly and efficiently. In the subsequent extraordinary and countrywide consolidation process, the ailing banks were closed, taken over, or merged.

As a consequence, the Swiss bank landscape changed dramatically. In the course of years from 1991 to 1995, the number of Swiss banks decreased from 625 to 413. Among the victims were the mentioned SVB with assets of SFr. 46.5 BLN and three cantonal banks. The Cantonal Bank of Berne with bad loans of SFr. 2.7 BLN was clinically dead but saved by the taxpayers. Until today, the number of all Swiss banks has dropped to 320, and from the former 204 independent regional- and local banks only eighty-three operate still independently. Finally, after almost fifteen years, in December 2005, the 6.300 customers of the former bankrupt bank STL have received the last installment being part of a total 60.7% of their original savings. The surviving Swiss banks emerged reinforced from the banking crisis despite losses of over SFr. 42 BLN from bad loans since 1991.

However, despite the Swiss financial place was saved from blame and trouble the silent author and discoverer received neither any thanks nor any compensation for his time consuming homework. Instead, an excellent work certificate from the personnel manager. But this was a useless paper because in October 1993, his candidacy for a lucrative bank position failed again, due to libel information supplied by the Swiss bank's representatives. This was officially denied but when the author met accidentally the bank director of a medium sized independent Swiss bank but belonging to the Credit Suisse Group on October 15, 2001, willing to offer him a lucrative bank position he gave the author a letter stating "I can confirm that the form and way your candidature has been objected was never in line with the appropriate banking practice". Cynically was also the answer of the Swiss Bank's CEO to the author's letter mentioning some of Swiss Bank's wrongdoings prior his exile to Thailand in May 2003: "If you have not been able in the first years to prove the allegedly injustice in writing you must close this chapter". In fact it took the author nine years or four years too long to comply with Swiss law to prove in writing this illegally false information by the Swiss Bank's representatives. Needless to say that the illegal preventing to occupy a lucrative bank position until the author's exile had for him economically disadvantages. Further strange was also that the "CIO" who was originally against the mentioned bank project did not allow the author first to work in the bank. Nevertheless, he took in the author's absence the 32 page bank report and distributed it in his name throughout the Swiss Bank "as strictly confidential" where it was used also for other purposes.

> Although stealing of ideas and copying others' work is ethically and morally despicable and even against international and national rules like the Swiss Financial Analyst Association (SFAA) it was common practice in the Swiss Bank—but who cared about? No one of the Swiss financial place where envy, greed and ego are no exceptions and appropriate guidelines to behave correctly in the workplace are either missing or ignored. This is different in the Singapore financial place where strict regulations are maintained to keep its good reputation thus preventing any wrongdoings.

In the meantime, all Swiss Bank's decision makers from 1989 to 2003 era were gently dismissed or left the bank voluntarily. Learning from the past failures, a new management was formed in 2003.

Result: new value-added investment products and services were created as proposed in 1989/1992, the customer accounts increased sharply and at the end of 2004 the Swiss Bank achieved, with an increase of 42% historically the biggest net profit of SFr. 137.1 MLN, succeeded by another top result of SFr. 179 million in 2005. This is in contrast to the loss of over SFr. 100 MLN at the end of 1990 and the inferior results prior to the takeover through the Credit Suisse Holding in March 1990. The bad performance of the previous years also confirm the negative effects of scandal management, including forced silence, envy, greed, missed business and market opportunities and thus losing customer accounts, and departing of qualified staff.

2007 Swiss Bank's End of its Independence

The successful turnaround achieved by the new management after 248 years in 2003 was too late. In April 2006, Credit Suisse Holding decided to merge its five banking units, including Swiss bank into a newly founded Swiss Private Bank. This step and the dismissal of 200 bank employees were not surprising as the overlapping business activities of these five units did not develop any synergies instead they were competing with each other and producing red tape at high cost. In fact, with letters of April 2005 to some Swiss top bank managers including Credit Suisse the author mentioned that it is contra productive that each of these units operates with an expensive infrastructure and offering same services and same products. Thus hindering unified market presence to attract new customers. In September 2005 UBS acted first and merged its independent different bank units and sold it at the price of SFr. 5.6 billion to the Swiss Private Bank Bear by keeping a stake of 20% and management control of the new and enlarged undertaking. Result: The shareholder values of both banks increased substantially.

The same was true for the shares of Credit Suisse Holding with its new corporation which started to operate on January 1st, 2007, with headquarters at the fashionable Zurich Bahnhof Strasse (Railway Station Street for English wording) of the formerly Swiss bank. At the end of 2008 the five combined bank units had assets of 94 BLN Swiss francs under management versus 129 BLN Swiss francs at end of 2007. The welcomed customers are "the super rich and also the simple millionaires" according to the new CEO. Not welcomed are bank servants or just administrators on the payroll, but co-workers operating like entrepreneurs with ideas and international flair.

Result: Prior the Swiss bank's end it was most productive by creating many funny slogans to skillfully cover deficiencies. Therefore nobody believed the following few selected examples such as: "Cultivated Banking", "We are the leading bank in the investment research", "No one can copy our very strong company culture" "We are the private bank to satisfy the highest demands for 250 years" etc. Being not competitive the "World's best bank" was finally forced to merge.

People in Thailand compared to rich Switzerland

In Thailand where Buddhism is the state religion, Thais are taught virtues like ethics, morals, goodness, modesty, and helpfulness in their childhood. One of Buddha's teachings is also not to hang the heart on pieces of the World like wealth and reputation as diseased striving for possessions and feeding on reputation creates more suffering than happiness. In Switzerland, however the World's richest country according to a study of the World Bank dated December, 2005 many Swiss have not learned yet or have forgotten the above lessons. This is underlined by the president of the council of a Swiss village who embezzled some SFr. 100.000 and died suddenly in his office at the age of seventy in 2005. The same is true in the emirate Oman where a Swiss honorary consul at the age of seventy-eight received SFr. 143.000 for issuing illegally 134 visas and was condemned by the Swiss Federal Court in 2004. Worse was the case of a former Swiss Ambassador in Luxembourg who was condemned to more than three years prison sentence by the Swiss Federal Court in 2005 for qualified money laundering and other wrongdoings.

However, what all Swiss media countrywide strongly criticized were the exorbitant annual remunerations of the CEO of UBS amounting to SFr. 24 million and particularly of the CEO of Credit Suisse up to SFr. 90 MLN based on a new incentive plan 2006. This is worldwide more than any CEO in Europe, USA, and Japan received 2006 according to the *Tages Anzeiger* of May 8, 2006, by comparing the remunerations of top CEOs. Such self-enrichment was condemned as greed, bad taste, theft, against public sentiment, and contra productive as the record earnings of UBS and Credit Suisse in 2005 were not achieved by two top managers only. It was the result of excellent market conditions and of ten thousands of hardworking employees operating worldwide. Nevertheless, the Swiss top bankers' exorbitant salaries were rigorously defended by Mr. Mirabaud, president of the Swiss Banking Association (SBV). In an emotional speech at a meeting published in the *Tages Anzeiger* of September 14, 2006, he complained vehemently that in "Switzerland a fatal downward leveling is taking place!"

However, only Swiss top bankers living in ivory towers are not aware, that it is often easier and much more rewarding to work in a Swiss bank top position instead working hard in lower but responsible and challenging functions for the sake of the Swiss banks and its employers.

> The controversy over the Swiss bank's top salaries did widen the gap between the over dimensioned Swiss financial place generating big profits also from foreign tax evasion and the Swiss work place creating competitive products of high value. Consequently, the representatives of the machinery, electric and metal industrial organizations considered leaving the umbrella organization of the Swiss economy called "Economiesuisse". And Nicolas Hayek, top manager of Swiss Swatch Group intended to found an "Association of entrepreneurs". He also mentioned in the *Sonntags-Zeitung of the Tages Anzeiger* of June 11, 2006: "Such a body would far better defend the interests of the Swiss work place at risk slowly to disappear due to short sighted bank managers. Such arguments of the Swiss workplace and the domination of the Swiss financial place divided the Swiss economy mentioned the *NZZ* from May 28, 2006. But what are good entrepreneurs and top managers doing? They firstly take care of the company, its employees, shareholders and behaving also ethically correctly. Besides, they have moral obligations to the society by sponsoring cultural, educational and social institutions which is common practice in the United States.

In the meantime the above mentioned "short sighted bank managers" were not only "short sighted" but also greedy, arrogant, careless and showing little or no responsibility. Being blind and ignoring the warnings from different sources since 2005 they missed to get out in time from the real estate and mortgage business becoming a ticking time bomb. Instead they pumped up credit volumes multiple times with speculative derivatives producing a big bubble of hot air imploding 2008. The two biggest banks UBS and Credit Suisse of which UBS was safeguarded by the Swiss Government were particularly hit. Therefore the new and already replaced UBS president Kurer admitted: "that we have to come down from the horse". Nevertheless, at the Annual Meeting of 2008 the president of the Swiss Banking Association, Mr. Mirabaud, stated that "the Swiss financial place is still healthy". But the questions remain why the net profits of billions generated easily until 2007 mutated so quickly into losses of billions already in 2008.

The Swiss banking disaster was the catalyst for many Swiss workers not accepting anymore salary increases of just 2.8% net inflation since 2002 compared to 80% of the top management. Sector winners 2008 were again the bank employees with above average increases of 5.7% net inflation while the sector losers were the sales people with average salaries decreasing 4% since 2002. Therefore the Swiss organization "Travail Suisse" will start 2008/2009 a public referendum to regulate the top salaries. This subject was also on the agenda of the finance ministers at the G-20 meeting in NY on November 15, 2008. Germany's government has ruled already that in future no top manager will receive more than EURO 500.000 annually if he operates in a company having received state support.

Contrary to the turmoil abroad Thailand was spared from big losses but the 2008 downward trend of the World's economies did not spare the Thai stock market plunging 56% like everywhere. The reason may be the Thais' strong believe in Buddha's teaching strictly condemning envy, greed and ego. This is also the reason why the Thais are so friendly and pleasant when one is meeting and working with them while in Switzerland similar Christian virtues have been pushed much to the background. Thanks are also not common courtesy in the Swiss culture, but if a Thai receives help, he will not forget this even later. Besides, it is astonishing how Thais with small remuneration and under difficult conditions achieve the highest standards relating to crafts and services. This outstanding performance is achieved through excellent teamwork in manufacturing, construction and services. Result: Not hurt as much by the recession in the Western world and Japan, Thailand benefits from the continued foreign investments into the Thai economy. Therefore the Bath appreciated 2008 against the world's major currencies substantially. Consequently the present political unrest dividing Thais in pro and contra Thaksin camps did not adversely affect the strong Thai currency.

Although Thais are proud of their country and achievements, there is no trace of arrogance as Thais are happy if they can work and have enough means for a satisfactory living. Not so many Swiss who, for little work receive maximum remunerations, but still want more. The German poet, Friedrich Schiller 1759-1805, who loved Switzerland's natural beauties and who had also excellent knowledge of the Swiss people wrote in the dialogue between Swiss William Tell and his son, Walter: "Tis better, child, to have these glacier peaks behind one's back, than evil-minded men"! But what made Thailand famous? The country's natural beauties, the old culture, the agriculture resources, and particularly the friendly smiling, helpful and industrious Thai people!

Preface

What is the purpose and catalyst of the APPENDIX

The appendix is an update of events in Switzerland and abroad since the book was published for the first time 2006 providing more information and taking into account the feedback of many readers. The catalyst was the Swiss Prime Minister Samuel Schmid in his speech on the eve of the Swiss national anniversary of August 1st, 2008: "We need an open country with space for big ideas". However, experience learned that big ideas alone are not good per se and may lead even to disasters. In the past in Switzerland big and good ideas were realized by brilliant entrepreneurs in cooperation with industrious coworkers having community spirit and solidarity coupled with hard work. Today many large achievements do remember the Swiss pioneers of that time. Additionally income from the export of high quality products made by innovative Swiss companies in the watch,-pharmaceutical,-machinery,-building and electro industry made Switzerland rich and famous without natural resources.

These facts and the country's beauty attracted many tourists, companies and rich people benefiting from Switzerland's bank secrecy, tax shelters, political and economical stability. Therefore Swiss banks made and make billions of easy money from the illegal tax evasion of foreign tax dodgers mainly from countries having budget problems in the EU and the USA. Subsequently small Switzerland became an over dimensioned financial place and a play ground for overpaid greedy Swiss bankers. Lacking competition from foreign banks many Swiss banks overcharged their clients for services which foreign banks offer much better and cheaper. This is not surprising as tax dodgers and elderly people will hardly complain and ask questions.

In Thailand the author continued to study business and other literature and wrote books and comments for the newspapers. Of particular interests were the following articles published in the American business magazines 2005-2007.

Business Week May 23, 2005:
"Taking Risk to Extremes—Will derivatives causing a major blow-up in the world's credit market? And "The serving of the huge wave in global credit market was so far successful".

Business Week March 26, 2007
"Inside the Mortgage Crisis—The bad news are far from over".

Business Week March 26, 2007:
"Making Sense of the Mortgage Mess—Defaults are soaring and fear is on the march. How far will the pain spread"?

Business Week April 2, 2007:
"The Mortgage Mess—Beware of the Silent Second—Lenders may not know of Homeowners' additional Mortgages".

Fortune April 2, 2007:
"Dropping the Ball—How the credit rating agencies got in the middle of the sub prime-lending crisis".

Using derivatives in the US credit business was common practice since the 1980s but became uncontrollable when reaching volumes of trillions inviting crooks labeling ABS and MBS wrongly as prime. In fact derivates are like fertilizer if used normally it helps to grow the plants if misused and used too much they get destroyed.

By uncovering of the Swiss Banking crises in October 1991 the author set up a sophisticated analyzing system with low and maximum points showing the best and worst banks at a glance. It had been exiting to set up a similar system for the Swiss banks 2005 ignoring the above warnings. Particularly hit were the banks producing and selling at a large scale derivates and sophisticated structured products like UBS.

In the 2nd half of 2008 the World's economies turned into a recession forcing the banks worldwide to write off $963 BLN bad loans. UBS and Credit Suisse suffered triple digit losses and UBS which became a too big risk for the Swiss financial place was rescued by the Swiss Government. Simultaneously the countries of the European Union and the USA attacked stronger than ever the Swiss banking secrecy and were successful. First on February 19, 2009, by disclosing the names of 300 US tax dodgers breaching the Swiss banking secrecy for the first time. Later on March 13, 2009, by adopting the OECD Standards provoking questions how competitive the Swiss banks will be without the banking secrecy generating billions from tax dodgers? The future will give the answer!

The author
Martin Zumbuehl

VII.
APPENDIX

Switzerland – Big Ideas, Swiss Banking Secrecy Wishful Thinking

Not big ideas but good ideas, hard work and discipline do lead to success and maintain the good reputation

The success of Switzerland's work place is based on good ideas coupled with hard work of all participants true to the Asian values "To put the goods of society above that of the individual". Besides, by making products of higher added value becoming brand names they were selling well in the World markets. Due to the sustained working ethic the Swiss work place maintained its excellent reputation of which the young banking industry could also benefit. To protect the increasing money flows the Swiss banking secrecy was legalized 1934 and Switzerland's modest financial place developed to an over dimensioned banking industry where Swiss bankers make easy money from foreign tax dodgers. By hardly creating value added products but producing self made triple digit billion losses the Swiss financial place's reputation has suffered a lot losing also the confidence of many bank customers.

Community spirit and solidarity do create good ideas

In Switzerland and elsewhere good life has the effect of sweet poison pills making weak people lazy, arrogant and reform hostile which in turn create envy, greed and ego. Such bad virtues do generally grow where money is easily made being typically in the Swiss financial place. Consequently there is not always harmony between the Swiss work place representing industrious skilled laborers and the Swiss financial place representing bank employees enjoying good life. Therefore the wish of the Swiss Prime Minister Schmid to create big ideas cannot be realized in environments lacking harmony.

This is also in line with the former Prime Minister Josef Deiss in his speech on August 1st, 2004: "That the Swiss Confederation is lived out as an Envy-Confederation where only one thing is important: Monday I am, Tuesday I am, Wednesday I am and so on leading to an unhealthy egoism".

Big Ideas of being Failures
Merger of the car companies Daimler Benz and Chrysler – failed
The transatlantic marriage of the two large car producers on May 6, 1998, between the successful German partner Daimler/Benz and the unsuccessful US partner Chrysler was a big idea but ill-fated from the beginning. Such connections never work neither in a natural marriage nor in a work place with co-workers. In fact, Chrysler needed constant support by means of know how and cash of billions of EURO. The frustrated German shareholders demanded the "divorce" and Daimler/Benz's profitability was restored again but feels today the pain of the world's recession 2008-2009.

Swissair to become the 4th largest European Airline – failed
This big idea was only to show off and also a failure from the beginning as preparations were highly insufficient and critical experts were missing or not involved. Nevertheless, the 19 Swissair board members, top managers and representatives of the Swiss politic and economy were dreaming to create Europe's 4th largest airline. This target should be reached by purchasing battered airlines despite Swissair's weak financial condition 1996. Loaded with huge debts and losses of billions of SFr Swissair was grounded and went bankrupt 2001. However, as the misconduct and the biggest bankruptcy of Swissair was legally not a crime its 19 representatives were acquitted by the Swiss court.

ALLFINANZ – Bank and Insurance Services under one roof
– Takeover of Winterthur Insurance Co by Credit Suisse – failed
Long time Credit Suisse CEO L. Mühlemann hesitated to take over the insurance company in order to offer bank and insurance services under one banking roof. Finally, on December 9. 1997, he acquired the company by changing CS shares into those of Winterthur but it was too late as financier Ebner has already pushed the share prices up by 80%. The losers were the CS share holders as the ALLFINANZ idea became European wide a big disaster swallowing billions of SFr.

– Takeover of Dresdner Bank by the Allianz Insurance Co – failed
In 2001 it was a big and expensive idea too but failed as in the saturated and fragmented German financial place more than 2000 banks are still operating.

The takeover price of € 23 BLN was exorbitant and further losses of the Dresdner Bank swallowed additional billions of EURO. Finally, in August 2008, Allianz could sell the Dresdner Bank to the Commerzbank at the price of € 9.8 BLN forcing the new merged Commerzbank to dismiss 9000 employees and close 700 branches. But the merger of two weak partners did not pay off as month later of the merger the new Commerzbank disclosed single digit BLN losses and the German Government had to rescue the bank.

Good Ideas do lead to Successes
Merger of Ciba and Sandoz to Novartis – successful
Due to the merger of Ciba and Sandoz the new formed company Novartis became the world's second largest pharmaceutical group on December 23, 1996. All participants operated in close co-operation and under strict secrecy to realize this good idea. With a world market share of 4.5% Novartis exceeded the critical limit of 3%. The share prices rocketed also in the following year 1997 at the Swiss Stock Exchange by 54%.

Merger of the Swiss banks UBS and SBC to UBS – successful
Another good idea was the merger of the two biggest Swiss banks the Union Bank of Switzerland and the Swiss Bank Corporation to become UBS the Europe's largest bank on June 29, 1998. Total assets under management were SFr. 1.700 BLN and thus becoming also the world's largest asset manager. The new bank suffered 1998 from setbacks such as the Asian crises and the debacle with the LTCM Hedge Fund. Nevertheless, excellent management, ethical principles and motivated co-workers made UBS in the middle of 2007 to the best reputed and capitalized bank with a market value of SFr. 170 BLN and with assets under management of SFr 3.265 BLN. In 2008 UBS was safeguarded by the Swiss Government and lost completely its former glamour.

Fall of the "Holy Swiss Banking Secrecy" after 75 Years
Defended unsuccessfully by Switzerland
Attacked successfully by the USA and the EU

The Swiss banking secrecy was legalized 1934 to protect the capital inflow particularly after 1914 and the victims of the Nazi regime 1931-1945. Therefore it was a blessing for all participants but until today the Swiss banking secrecy helped mainly foreign tax dodgers to provide the Swiss banks with billions of cheap capital. By receiving such money from countries with budget problems the Swiss banks maximized their profitability and maintained its competitive advantage vs. foreign banks.

Therefore the Swiss banks were never prepared to give up this highly lucrative instrument. In fact in the course of years the Swiss banks accumulated worldwide assets under management of SFr. 5.235 BLN 2007 of which SFr 2.150 BLN in Switzerland alone. Of this sum the possible untaxed assets account for 42% from foreign private clients while 14.5% to 20.5% of taxed assets are from foreign institutional investors. In the case that "only SFr 1.000 BLN" would break away, a quarter of bankers, investment advisers, layers and others could lose their jobs partly reducing the over dimensioned financial place and negatively impacting Switzerland's prosperity.

Since 1934 the Swiss banking secrecy enabled the Swiss bankers, nicknamed abroad "financial jugglers", to enjoy a comfortable life. By poaching in the foreign tax income substance the Swiss financial place received legally cheap easy money from the illegal foreign tax evasion. Thus the banking secrecy was a source of good life promoting laziness, hindering progress and making "fat and impotent" as stated by a well known private banker in his biography of 2004. In fact it was ethically and morally a shame to take money from countries where it is urgently needed while their complaints were arrogantly ignored and rejected for decades. Therefore Swiss banks have lost reputation, goodwill and got threats from the suffering countries with budget problems. In the following quoted excerpts taken from the US magazine Time of September 16, 2002 and other sources underline this statement:

The following quoted excerpts taken from the US magazine Time of September 16, 2002 and other sources underline this statement:

> "Silence is golden – the Swiss banking industry is trying to improve its image. But it still wants to keep mum about accounts held by European residents.

The Swiss will inevitably be portrayed as profiting from the proceeds of what everyone else thinks of as a crime".

And Swiss private banker J. Bear mentioned in an interview with the Swiss newspaper *"Weltwoche"* in spring 2004 "the banking secrecy is damaging the country's reputation considerably particularly as for institutional investors like pension funds the banking secrecy is of no importance". The increasing criticism from abroad confirms the former German finance minister Eichel in February 2008 calling Switzerland the "biggest brake-block to stop tax evasion. Besides, in November 2008 he stated: "The Swiss banking secrecy is no business model for the future".

Therefore the answer of the Swiss Finance Minister Merz in March, 2008, to the address of the EU was shortsighted: "the Swiss banking secrecy is not negotiable", "When biting the banking secrecy you will lose your teeth". Almost intimidating his statement in September 2008, "Hollowing the banking secrecy is punishable as it is an official crime". Soon after these aggressive and not wisely remarks proved contra productive already on February 18, 2009, as the US tax authority were forcing UBS to send a confidential list of 300 supposed US tax dodgers thus breaching for the first time the Swiss banking secrecy. Besides, the German tax officials managed to get access to the data of rich German tax dodgers having accounts with Liechtenstein's banks. This made the president of the Swiss Banking Association very angry by calling it "Gestapo Methods". Valuable information provided also a former UBS manager disclosing how rich US customers were advised to evade US taxes. The subsequent excuse of the UBS and the promise to waive off in future the off-shore business was also a defeat of the Swiss financial place. Additionally UBS was fined $150 MLN and Credit Suisse $15 MLN plus full compensation to their customers for selling Auction Rate Securities (ARS) based also on students loans as excellent and stable investments becoming worthless.

OECD Standards replace the "Holy Swiss Banking Secrecy"
After the historical breakthrough of the US Tax Authorities to disclose a confidential list of 300 US citizens having Swiss accounts the Swiss financial place was put again under pressure by the members of the *OECD* called *Organization of Economic Cooperation and Development*. The latter were preparing a black list of non cooperative countries including Switzerland opposing to give up the banking secrecy. As a result another breakthrough followed on March 13, 2009, as Swiss Finance Minister Merz and an irritated Swiss Government made

worldwide headlines that Switzerland was finally ready to give up its former banking secrecy. Simultaneously other tax heavens such as Liechtenstein, Luxemburg, Austria Andorra and Monaco have adopted the OECD Standards incl. automated exchange of information and waiving off the banking secrecy.

The most important element of the OECD Standards is that not only tax fraud is a crime but also tax evasion enabling tax authorities to force the banks to disclose data of proven tax dodgers. Tax evasion under the former Swiss banking secrecy was never a crime and thus fiscal data were not available to any Tax Authority. But for Swiss citizens and foreigners with domicile in Switzerland the banking secrecy was no subject as the Swiss tax authorities do not receive any information from the banks.

Thus the taxpayers enjoy a "confidence bonus" by submitting the tax documents to the Swiss tax authorities for the assessment. But in the case the tax authority discover a tax evasion the culprit will be charged substantially with additional taxes plus a heavy fine. However, in the case of tax fraud being the falsification of tax documentation or providing intentional wrong information the tax dodger will face a criminal procedure at the Swiss court.

However, as the above cited countries were prepared to adopt the OECD Standards incl. automated exchange of information Switzerland still makes conditions and wants a number of concessions. First it will revise with 70 countries the existing withholding tax agreements of which some need the approval of the parliament. Besides, Switzerland refuses to give the automated exchange of information, will deliver only fiscal information on case by case and tax fraud must be founded and well documented. Therefore it will take years until the new OECD Standard will become operative. The question will be whether the OECD members will accept Switzerland's special wishes.

The Swiss government's stubbornness and the back and forward "strategy" was contra productive as this little country had earned much more respect if it had been in line with the OECD from the beginning. Consequently system analyst Denis Meadows's interview published in the NZZ of November 3, 2008, describes perfectly the Swiss mentality "It is time that Switzerland forgets the idea sitting on a small mountain and observing and ignoring the problems abroad. It is not anymore like in World War II when people everywhere killed each other while the country remained unhurt. At that time Switzerland was lucky and clever for not being involved. In future this will not be possible anymore".

2009 Rescuing of the Swiss Bank UBS by the Government

After 2002 the US discount rate decreased gradually to historic lows of 1% generating abundant liquidity in the markets. All banks incl. UBS and Credit Suisse benefited from the real estate boom. Driven by greed and derivatives credit volumes were pumped up multiple times. But many market players realized too late that they financed mainly hot air with billions of dollars. As a result UBS and Credit Suisse suffered in the first eight months triple digit losses.

UBS was particularly hit and disclosed losses of SFr 48 BLN. In October 2008 the UBS President Kurer admitted further "toxic assets" of SFr 68 BLN wiping off the bank's equity. But worse was the withdrawal of customers' assets of SFr 226 BLN. Having no other choice the Swiss Government rescued Switzerland's biggest bank which became a too big risk for the Swiss financial place. Finally the President Kurer was replaced by the former CEO of Credit Suisse. Needless to say that the shares of Credit Suisse and UBS plunged to record lows. Thus resulting in a self made contracting of the Swiss market capitalization.

Wishful Thinking – Swiss Financial Place should join World's Champions- League?

Among the few tax shelters worldwide the Swiss financial place is by far the largest one. However, what do foreign banks much better that they can operate successfully without the banking secrecy? Such a question no one would dare to ask as the "Swiss financial place should be a world leader also in research and teaching" said the president of the Swiss banking association (SBV). Therefore he would never admit that the Swiss banks are seemingly not competitive enough.

The competitiveness of the Swiss financial place has also been questioned and tested by the World Economic Forum (WEF) classifying the Swiss financial place as not transparent on rank 7 and the Swiss banks being little efficient on rank 27— behind South Africa, Japan and slightly before Vietnam on the world's banking list of September 12, 2008. The fact that these countries can operate without the banking secrecy the WEF rankings are still flattering as the Swiss banks have the worst cost/earnings ratios compared to 15 banks in the EU stated the Consulting Office Arthur D and published in the TA of 18.12.2007.

In fact, few countries worldwide offer the banks such good economic conditions plus the banking secrecy like Switzerland. This is not the case for many banks in Asia, Africa, South America and other emerging countries operating not always under optimal economic conditions and without the banking secrecy. Nevertheless, these banks are competitive as hard work and business ethics do promote flexibility, creativity and productivity. Consequently the dream of certain top bankers that the Swiss financial place should become number 3 behind the financial places of New York and London is wishful thinking.

Necessity is the mother of invention
Necessity also promotes creativity and productivity. Consequently it is not surprising that in the course of years the different and indifferent banking business of most of the 320 Swiss banks has little changed. In fact part of the bankers go day by day in the office with the same professional knowledge acquired many years go while the banking secrecy favors indirectly laziness because competition is limited. Therefore the bank customers pay substantially for services which are better and cheaper abroad. In the case of asset management high management fees are also the rule. And should an investor suffering from loses because his portfolio highly underperformed the market is blamed despite it was often the result of lacking professional skills.

Conclusion
In the over dimensioned Swiss financial place Swiss bankers generate easy money thanks to the money flow of tax dodgers using the banking secrecy. Therefore the salaries of the Swiss bankers are substantially above average compared to their foreign bank colleagues despite they are better qualified and thus offering better service. This is not surprising as easy money and good life do not oblige or motivate to increase professional knowledge but triggering off envy and greed if other coworkers have good ideas and make a better job.

Worse are bankers with academician background without practical skills being arrogant and always right despite being wrong not admitting errors and being reform hostile. Such people are more a burden than an asset and a lesson for employers to investigate their university degrees. Covering up their weaknesses is the catalyst to start wrongdoings. Therefore they should be stopped before getting promoted. As a result it will take a long time to restore the bad reputation of the Swiss financial place. Besides, the formerly secure Swiss banking secrecy being mainly an instrument for tax dodgers was anyway not "water proof" anymore.

Therefore they may look for other bank relations offering better and cheaper services. This assumption is supported by the *"New York Times"* in January 2009 as follow: "There is no security to transfer money in countries with and without the banking secrecy. If you give the money in the hands of god knows financial experts in Zurich, you can give it also to someone god knows what he is doing with it".

Finally the presently battered car- and bank industries in the United States, Europe and Japan and the chapters of this book have disclosed and the experience has learned that a company or a bank can recover only in line with the quality of its board members, CEO, managers, co-workers and employees. Therefore it is much easer to go the rural way of life leading from the darkness to a brighter and better future by having the virtues and knowledge detailed below.

Company Profile
C – Character – Confidence in the management
C – Credibility – Credit- and trustworthy versus banks, buyers/sellers
C – Capability – Capable to manage successfully a company

Manager- and Coworker Profile
C – Character – honest, correct, integer, free of influence, not corrupt
C – Credibility – trustworthy versus third parties, showing responsibility
C – Capability – capable, independent, innovative, flexible, cooperative,
                         able working under pressure

The Author
Martin Zumbuehl

VIII.
Sources of Information

I. Introduction

Spanish Court decision:
"Six month prison for husband for spying wife's electronic box",
TA* of June 16, 2005
Sarbanes-Oxley Act:
"It is easier for staff uncovering bosses' wrongdoings",
Business Week of March 25, 2006
Cleaning up Boeing:
"End of culture of silence, reward for real performance",
Business Week of March 13, 2006

II. Swiss Justice

German wording of the case of Mrs. X
German wording of the Federal Court decision of June 8, 2005
Official comments to different legal articles of harassment:
"Clear definitions of the Federal Court are missing"
"Public discussions have become seldom",

Violation of human rights in Switzerland:
Condemnation of two Swiss journalists
TA* of April 26, 2006
"Switzerland is a "champion" in int. human rights"
"As appropriate instance is missing",
NZZ** of May 14, 2006
"No one must accuse himself for tax evasion",
TA* of September 26, 2006

Opinion of a Swiss financial expert:
"Member of Council of State FL – was charged with speeding",
TA* of July 2005

III. Swiss Life

Too much of good life makes people lazy,
"Swiss firms are lazy" from Zehnder & Partner,
TA* of September 30, 2004
"Slow growth of Swiss economy worried again the OECD",
NZZ** of January 6, 2006
"US ethic enforcers maintain corporate governance",
Business Week of February 13, 2006
"Many Swiss have lower income today than in the 1990s",
TA* of August 31, 2008
*"Swiss economy in the purgatory", NZZ** of November 10, 2002*
*"The crook in the office", NZZ** and TA* of August 10, 2005*
"Who is afraid of the whistleblowers", TA of August 5, 2005*
"My lord give us power for reforms", Swiss Revue of July, 2005
Swatch founder Nicolas G. Hayek:
"Switzerland needs entrepreneurs again",
Swiss Revue of August 2005
"Destroying judgment for Switzerland", OECD
NZZ** of March 1, 2005

IV. Swiss and Foreign education

Swiss education:
"Swiss universities are mainly occupied with themselves",
Weltwoche of December 16, 2005
"University teaching needs a quality offensive",
Weltwoche of December 4, 2004
"Innovation is the A and O to survive", Zehnder & Partner,
TA* of September 30, 2004
*"Govern in Switzerland means good and circumvent
administration",*
"Too much red type is dominating the public administration"
Swiss People Party Meeting August 19, 2006

English education:
"Oxford has some problems but wants to solve it"
Business Week of December 5, 2005
"US students discover British universities,
Business Week of September 25, 2006

US education:
"What makes the difference of American and Chinese teaching?"
News Week of August 28, 2006
"Excerpts of reports of Survey Higher education",
The Economist of September 10. 2005
"B-Schools: Only a C in Ethics",
Business Week of September 5/12, 2005

V. Swiss and Foreign Finance
Swiss finance:
"Financial place should lead the world in research and teaching",
NZZ* of August 30, 2005
"Swiss employees have become less productive",
BAK*** of November 2, 2004
"In which bank division Swiss employees make the most money?"
Excerpts from different sources of 2005-2006
"Hardly all of 8000 supervised pension funds are well managed",
TA* of September 13, 2006

English finance:
"Who are the rich customers of the Swiss banks?"
Forbes, Global of May 23, 2005
"Listing of the Russian oil company Rosneft at the LSE",
NZZ** of July 18, 2006

Singapore Finance:
"How did the financial place develop?"
Time Magazine of December 12, 2005

2005-2006 Rise of Citigroup:
"Implementation of rules of conduct",
Bangkok Post of February 18, 2005

2007-2008 Fall of Citigroup
"Implementation of business guidelines & strategies"
Citigroup's Annual Report 2007

Conclusion of Swiss and foreign finance:
"A quarter of Swiss bank employees do not feel well in the office"
TA* of January 28, 2006
"Is your workplace psychologically healthy?"
The Pattaya Mail of March 17, 2006
"Uncovering of wrongdoings is treason of internal affairs",
Swiss money cab of September 2005
"Privacy is important for mankind",
"Advertisement of Swiss private banks",
NZZ** of 2001
"Swiss MP RG: Whistleblowers should be protected by law",
Swiss Blick of September22, 2005
"In Switzerland a big necessity exits to uncover wrongdoings",
NZZ* of October 9, 2006

VI. Swiss and foreign Ethics and Morals

According to Buddha:
"*Decay of good manners leads to delusion*",
Weltwoche of August 6, 2005
"*In 2015 Asia contributes 45% of the world's GDP*",
The Economist of March 18, 2006

Teaching of Buddha and Teaching of Christianity:
"*In the Envy-Confederation community spirit is lost*",
Swiss Prime Minister Deiss speech of August 1, 2006

The power of Asian values:
"*German excerpts of the book Japan vs. China*",
Weltwoche of July 2005

The power of Western values:
"*The rise of entrepreneurs and Virtue's Intermediaries*",
The Economist of February 25, 2006

1989-2003 Swiss Bank's Violation of Rules and Conduct & Ethics. "*What is the meaning of EQ*"?
Pattaya Mail of June 9, 2006

South Korean working ethics:
"*The secrets of the turnaround*",
Magazine Fortune of September 5, 2005

People in Thailand compared to rich Switzerland:
"*Swiss work place and Swiss financial place drift away*",
TA* of June 11, 2006
"*Entrepreneurship must regain reputation*",
TA* of May 28, 2006
"*A fatal downward leveling of salaries is taking place*",
TA* of September 14, 2006

What is the purpose of the APPENDIX?
"*Taking Risks to Extremes–Will derivatives causing a blow-up*"
Business Week, May 23, 2005

APPENDIX
"*It's time that Suisse forgets the idea sitting on a small mountain*"
Interview of Marco Metzler with System Analyst D. Meadows,
NZZ of November 3, 2008

TA*   Swiss Tages Anzeiger
NZZ** Swiss Neue Zürcher Zeitung
BAK*** Swiss Basel Economics AG